Praise for
VIRGINIA O'HARE'S INTERNATIONAL BEST SELLER

VIRGINIA O'HARE DOCUMENTS GOD'S LAW VS. MAN'S LAW

*"**Other than the Bible, this new book is the #1 MUST READ for every single American!** I have never met anyone as intelligent, determined, and dedicated as Virginia O'Hare. Her book will have a tremendous impact on all those who want to see our Civil and Constitutional Rights upheld by our Government. With her God-given strength, she will see that justice is served for her son."*

Brenda Spiwak
Charity Fundraiser
South Florida

*"Virginia, I just finished reading this amazing and powerful book! I am so deeply moved. **Just thinking of all you and your son have been through is unimaginable!** I pray that your deep, your faith will continue to keep you strong. You and Robert are always in my thoughts."*

Lois A. Stoll
Vice President / Sr. Business Development Officer
Banking Industry

*"When I read Virginia's first book, **Virginia O'Hare's Trials, Triumphs, and Vision from God,** I said that I could not put it down because it was so gripping, and it created a desire in me to see how it ended. Her new book, **Virginia O'Hare Documents God's Laws vs. Man's Laws,** affects me in a very different way. This book has kept me from being able to get the subject out of my conscience. No matter what I think or do, God's laws continue to pop-up in my mind.*

This book is so important for those of us trying to cope with today's crazy world. It is a Biblical guide that is written with great clarity and Godly inspiration. This is a book that all Christians should read if they truly want to understand the difference between man's laws and God's laws.

Most of us have gone through life, not fully understanding what influence the evil one has had on mankind's laws. The laws of government may have started out under the influence of God's laws, but they have been twisted and changed for man's purpose. As a student of history, the law, and the Bible, Virginia brings it all together by sharing her real-life experiences and her faith. I believe whoever reads this book will have similar feelings, and their faith will be positively affected for the rest of their life."

Vincent J Vella CFP®
Senior Vice President
Wealth Management Advisor

ISBN: 978-0-578-80190-2

Book Cover and Interior Design by Kristine Cotterman
Exodus Design Studio
www.ExodusDesign.com

First printing: 2020

Printed in the United States of America

VIRGINIA O'HARE

In Memory of Patty Lynne

My darling daughter, Patty Lynne,
I cherish the mother-daughter bond we shared in our earthly life.
I was truly blessed having you, Anne Marie, and Robert Anthony
as my three most cherished gifts from God.
I know soon we will all be reunited in Christ,
as a family, and will rejoice together in Heaven forever!

"This is what the Lord,
the God of Israel, says:
Write in a book all the words
I have spoken to you."
Jeremiah 30:2 (NIV)

TABLE OF CONTENTS

DEDICATION

I dedicate this book to God the Father,
God the Son,
and God the Holy Spirit.

It is in loving memory of my husband, Dan, and children,
Anne Marie, Patty Lynne, and Robert Anthony,
who have passed through death's door to their glorious
destiny of eternal salvation through Jesus Christ,
who is more powerful than death and time.

On September 17, 2012, my eldest daughter
Anne Marie, fifty-four years old,
went home to be with the Lord.

On September 30, 2013, my husband and soul mate,
Daniel R. Ortung, seventy-five years old,
went home to be with the Lord.

On November 25, 2013, my youngest daughter,
Patricia Lynne, fifty-four years old,
went home to be with the Lord.

On July 27, 2020, my beloved son,
Robert Anthony, fifty-eight years old,
went home to be with the Lord.

PREFACE

Best-selling author, Virginia O'Hare, published her first book on August 28, 2014, titled *"Virginia O'Hare's Trials, Triumphs and Vision From God."* The book documented her miraculous vision from God. One evening, while standing alone on the bridge next to her home in Ft. Lauderdale, Florida, she heard a thunderous speaking voice coming from the sky. She looked up and saw and heard God speaking to her, saying: ***"Virginia, in you, I am well pleased. I have chosen you to be My last day prophet. Through you, 10 x 10 million souls will be saved."*** Hearing and seeing God's overwhelming presence, caused her to question, *"Am I really seeing and hearing this?"* Knowing her thoughts, He said, ***"So that you know this is from Me, your picture will be on the front page of the newspaper."***

Soon thereafter, Virginia's picture was on the front page of the Fort Lauderdale Sun-Sentinel newspaper. The article covered over 20 percent of the top portion of the front page, fueled by her recent award-winning medical malpractice lawsuit in the New York Supreme Court. A jury unanimously ruled against a renowned New York doctor for not using acceptable medical standards in performing an abdominoplasty on Virginia and causing her severe bodily harm, and disfigurement. He performed an abdomino-plasty for medical reasons, to tighten muscles in the abdominal wall weakened by three successive childbirths.

On that fateful day, the doctor commenced his surgical procedure cutting into Virginia's abdomen without giving her the proper amount of sedation. She could feel the knife cutting across her body as he made incisions across her abdomen and around both hips. Being tightly strapped to the operating table, and unable to move, she screamed, *"Doctor, Stop! I can feel the knife cutting across my body."* He didn't stop. He kept cutting across her abdomen, while yelling to his surgical assistant, *"give her more sedation!"* He did not visit Virginia until the morning of the 7th day after surgery. He rushed into her room, complaining, *"You keep calling my office! Well, I'm here now to remove your bandages."* In one sweep, he abruptly ripped off the large bandages that covered her entire abdomen, and said, as he slapped his cold hand on her abdomen, *"Now you have a nice sexy belly."* Then he hurried out of the room, leaving Virginia alone to view his surgical blunder left on her body. She screamed in total shock upon viewing the large, jagged, uneven, and unsutured wounds across her lower abdomen and around both hips. Her belly button was also partially unsutured and 2 ½" off-center. Blood was pouring down her legs from all the open wounds. The medical staff, who were down the hall, could hear her screaming. They ran into her room and gasped upon viewing her grossly carved up body. They rebandaged her entire abdomen to stop the flow of blood from her opened, gaping wounds, then heavily sedated her.

On May 21, 1979, Virginia O'Hare won a landmark jury verdict in the New York Supreme Court for $854,000. **Dr. Howard Bellen was found liable for committing medical malpractice, and not using acceptable medical standards in performing the abdominoplasty surgery on his patient**. The jury's award created worldwide notoriety for Virginia. Talk show hosts like Johnny Carson, Merv Griffin, and countless other celebrities kept commenting about this compelling medical malpractice award and thought it was a lot of money for an off-centered belly button. This award was taken out of context by the news media and not viewed in the serious manner it was. Game show contestants were asked, *"What did Virginia O'Hare receive $854,000 for?"* Top-selling magazines featured her medical malpractice victory on their front pages. One TV news reporter stated, *"Only 20 minutes after Virginia O'Hare's jury verdict and award of $854,000 was announced, over $20,000,000 was spent on advertising her world-famous award."* Such news media frenzy continued unabated for years causing Virginia to make major life changes to protect her family.

Her first book also covered her marriage of 13 years to a correction officer, which produced three beautiful children. Unfortunately, the marriage was doomed from the beginning with violent domestic spousal abuse. At 33 years of age, her divorce became final and freed her and her children from all the physical, emotional, and psychological trauma they had been living with. The divorce was a blessing. She now had the sole responsibility to raise and support their three young children, 9,11,12, as a single parent, with very limited funds. The love and support from her children, family, friends, and her strong faith in God motivated her to move forward. The ink on her divorce papers was not dry when she opened her Employment Agency, O'Hare Personnel, in Poughkeepsie, NY. Several months later, her earnings from the newly established business, tripled the total yearly income of her ex-husband. Thereafter, her profits substantially grew each and every year for nine years, until she sold the Employment Agency.

At 42 years of age, the spotlight from her world-famous, record-breaking, medical malpractice lawsuit caused her to sell both her home in Poughkeepsie, NY, which she had built for her three children and her successful employment agency. She moved her family to Fort Lauderdale, FL, to start a new life.

After settling her family into an apartment, Virginia went to real estate school and got her Florida real estate license, and successfully developed a career, listing and selling multi-million dollar waterfront properties in upscale communities. From her first year and each year thereafter, she maintained a #1 top producer status, which allowed her to independently support her three children and grow her real estate business into earnings of multi-millions of dollars. She never acknowledges such wealth belonged to her. She felt whatever she earned belonged to God and that she was only the steward of such wealth.

Shortly after starting her new career in Real Estate, Virginia purchased a waterfront home on a scenic point lot in an upscale community in Fort Lauderdale, Fl. for her family, which was next to a bridge. This is where she had the audible and visual apparition of God while standing alone on the bridge next to her home. She treasured the vision in her heart and went forward working successfully in her real estate business until many years later, when she reached the age of 77. She lost her second husband of 45 years and her two daughters, both 54 years old. They all passed away within one year and 55 days of each other. She was left with a broken heart and her only surviving son, Robert Anthony.

Included in her first book, are the original trial transcripts from the world-famous medical malpractice trial, which she had sealed as part of her settlement agreement. She knew that one day, she would write her own story and clear up all the misconceptions surrounding her famous malpractice lawsuit that was erroneously portrayed by the news media. Many readers and critics stated, after reading her compelling life story, that they wanted the book to go on and read more about her life. Unfortunately for her, they got their wish. **One year after the book was published in 2014, tragedy struck her life again.** She details the horrible devastation she and her son, Robert Anthony, went through in her second book titled, *"Virginia O'Hare Documents God's Laws vs. Man's Laws."* On December 22, 2018, her self-published became an instant best-seller, with soaring sales and five-star rating on Amazon, Walmart, Good Reads, and countless other publication medias.

The subject matter of this all-inspiring second book was to document God's laws vs. Man's laws and expose the tragedy that struck her and her son's life. Their tragic story began on October 5, 2015, when her son Robert Anthony, was brutally assaulted inside their 2nd home in Mt. Dora, Florida by three Lake County deputy sheriffs. They unlawfully forced their way into her home without a search warrant or probable cause. Then, without any provocation, the three deputies brutally assaulted her son in front of her. The beating left him traumatized with serious bodily injuries. Their criminal violations included an unlawful search and seizure, staging of a phony crime scene in their home, filing a false police report, and making a false arrest charge against Robert Anthony for resisting an officer without violence.

The three deputies' criminal acts were formerly documented by the Lake County judge in his order to Robert Anthony's motion to suppress. He stated the deputies' actions were unlawful. However, in error, the judge gave a non-applicable case law of inevitable discovery in favor of the three deputies in his order and denied Robert Anthony's legal right to his motion to suppress. On appeal, the Florida appellate court overturned the judge's order and remanded the case back to the Lake County courts. Unfortunately, the Lake County Florida judge, the Lake County prosecutor, and the Lake County sheriff disagreed and exonerated the deputies' criminal violations, and ignored her son's civil and constitutional rights. Thereafter, events that occurred further violated Robert Anthony's constitutional rights and catapulted their life into a living nightmare.

Not finding justice for her son in the Lake County court system, Virginia filed complaints with the U.S. Attorney General, the FBI, and President Donald J. Trump. Her formal complaints included:

names of witnesses, pictures, a live video of the aftermath of the deputies' brutal beating, police body-worn camcorder audio, deputies' depositions, which documented their false statements made under oath during court proceedings.

While not honoring her son's legal rights, the Lake County, and later, the Marion County Detention Centers in Florida, kept him incarcerated for a total of 1011 days. During this time, they violated his civil, constitutional, and prisoner's rights and caused him to go without urgently needed medical care and treatment for his stage four colon cancer. There were over 550 pages of her son's medical and surgical records as proof he was being denied urgently needed medical care and treatment while incarcerated. He lost his rights as an American citizen, his health, his colon, and after an emergency colostomy, he faced a death sentence from stage four colon cancer that metastasized throughout his vital organs and lymph glands.

Robert's four lawyers, with full knowledge of the corruption and conspiracy by the officers, and the Lake County Judicial System had Robert plead no contest and appealed rather than go to trial under such bias and political conditions. On February 1, 2019, Robert Anthony won a reversal and remand order from the Fifth District Court of Appeals in Florida. Still not wanting to free Robert, the Lake County sheriff assigned one of the three deputies who had assaulted Robert on October 5, 2015, to investigate Robert's jail calls with his mother. They often spoke to each other in code. The deputy pulled out two words from the code and put them together to read: "kill" and "Briggs," and charged Robert with a new charge of solicitation to murder presiding judge, Don Briggs. Thereafter, Judge Briggs was immediately recused by State Attorney, Bradley King. These two words were never spoken on any monitored jail calls, nor was there any such evidence of this outrageous charge being perpetrated. On May 9, 2019, another judge from Lake County, released Robert on medical bail while awaiting-his pending Appeal. The Marion and Lake County facilities are under the supervision of Florida State Attorney, Bradley King, who Virginia personally spoke to and formally updated him on all the violations committed against her son's civil and constitutional rights by employees under his supervision. He never took any affirmative action on her formal complaint, nor honored her son's constitutional rights until Robert's stage 4 colon cancer was diagnosed as terminal. On the 2nd of March 2020, State Attorney, Brad King dropped the charges against Robert and signed a Nolle Prosequi order.

Robert Anthony's 1,011 days of incarceration caused his medically untreated stage four malignant colon cancer to grow and completely block his entire colon, which became life-threatening. His cancer led to unbearable pain and suffering, and the loss of almost 80 pounds. On April 17, 2019, the Marion County Detention Center had Robert rushed to the hospital in Ocala, Florida, to remove his entire cancerous colon, a surgery that was necessary to save his life. The surgeon warned Robert of his serious life-threatening condition, stating: *"If you had come to the hospital one day later, you would be dead. The tumor had completely blocked your entire colon and was emptying your bile into your body. I had to remove the entire colon, and I still couldn't remove all of the cancer cells. They are still in your lymph nodes, rectum, and other organs. You have stage four colon cancer that will soon take your life."*

Robert Anthony had to deal with wearing a colostomy bag on his stomach, to empty his bowels, and the dire medical prognosis of cancerous cells still spreading to his lymph nodes, lungs, rectum, and other vital organs. Upon his release on bond, May 19, 2019, Robert Anthony was treated at the Holy Cross Medical Center in Ft. Lauderdale, and the world-renowned Cleveland Clinic. He was further diagnosed with a 7-centimeter mass growth in his rectum-which is life-threatening.

On September 13, 2019, Virginia O'Hare filed a civil rights lawsuit on behalf of her son in Federal Court against all the entities involved in violating her son's civil, constitutional, and prisoner rights.

On October 17, 2019, Robert Anthony was taken to the ER at Imperial Point Hospital in Ft. Lauderdale, Fl. with a painful bowel obstruction. The Surgeon said the cancer had spread throughout his abdominal area, and his CT scan lit up like a Christmas tree. He gave Robert 1-3 months to live.

On December 20, 2019, Robert's lawyers were forced to file a THIRD APPEAL with the Fifth District Court of Appeal of Florida. After winning two successful Orders of Reversal from the Appellate Court, each time the case was remanded back to the lower court for retrial and each time, the lower court again ruled against Robert. Now after Robert received a THIRD RULING AGAINST HIM, with what amounts to the highly unconstitutional act of "DOUBLE JEOPARDY," Robert's legal team has filed a "DIVINELY INSPIRED," and absolutely brilliant, Initial Brief that should end this matter once and for all and set Robert free, and allow him to live out his remaining time as a FREE MAN! This incredible document has been included in the Appendix of this book for you to see and read for yourselves, the God-given words that will **finally free Robert!**

In addition to dealing with the tragedy against her son, Virginia was still suffering the heartache and loss of her two daughters, Anne Marie, Patty Lynne, and her husband of 45 years, Daniel Ortung. They all passed away within 14 months of each other. Anne Marie passed away on September 17, 2012. Daniel passed away on September 30, 2013. Patty Lynne passed away 55 days later, on November 25, 2013. After memorializing their life during a public service in Mt. Dora, FL, Virginia sold their Mt. Dora home and moved back to her Ft. Lauderdale residence on November 17, 2017.

One morning, while pondering the subject for her third book, the Holy Spirit prompted Virginia to look through a large armoire where her family's cremated remains were stored. She found Patty Lynne's handwritten manuscript with a card on top of her manuscript, that read: ***"This is what the Lord, the God of Israel says: 'Write in a book all the words I have spoken to you'"* (Jeremiah 30:2 NIV)**. Virginia felt compelled to include Patty Lynne's inspired manuscript in her latest book titled, *"Virginia O'Hare Declares God's Final Warning to the World."* Virginia's three books are spiritually inspired and include scriptures from both the Old and New Testaments with pictures of her beloved family.

INTRODUCTION

In fulfillment of Bible Prophecy, are two major prophetic signs of the Last Days that have been fulfilled in our generation. On May 14, 1948, Israel officially became a nation after being exiled for nearly 2000 years. On November 1, 1952, the United States' conducted its first nuclear test of a fusion device, or hydrogen bomb, at Enewetak in the Marshall Islands, which yielded 10 megatons of TNT, 1000 times larger than the bomb dropped on Hiroshima. On November 22, 1955, the Soviet Union exploded its first hydrogen bomb. It had a yield of 1.6 megatons. Several years later, on October 23, 1961, their hydrogen bomb tests culminated with explosions of approximately 58 megatons.

In the years that followed, there was a race among the nations of the world to stockpile these weapons of mass destruction, which opened the door to end all life from this planet. If all the nuclear weapons in the world were detonated at once, civilization would collapse. Jesus warned, *"Unless those days were shortened, no flesh would be saved; but for the elect's sake, those days will be shortened"* (Matthew 24:22 NKJV). Jesus also warned once these final signs occur, the generation alive at that time, *"will by no means pass away till all these things take place"* (Matthew 24:34 NKJV). We are the generation that is witnessing the fulfillment of all these biblical End-of Days signs and wonders that will bring an end to Satan's rulership of this world and herald in the second coming of Jesus who will establish God's Kingdom here on earth (see 2 Timothy 3:1). Then, death, sin, and everything evil will be swallowed up forever and replaced with total peace, joy, and happiness in the kingdom of God! (see 1 Corinthians 15:54)

Two thousand years ago, Jesus gave his disciples natural and supernatural signs that would precede his second coming. **These prophetic signs are happening now!** Our world is reeling from unprecedented disasters increasing with frequency and intensity. Crime and corruption are exploding everywhere. There is an earth-shaking spiritual warfare that is intensifying against our generation like never before. This is causing mega chaos and disasters to lives and property across the globe. Anarchy exists around the world, and poorly run governments are operating against the welfare of the people, and diminishing their rights and freedoms. This is affecting families and communities everywhere. Satan, knowing he has a short time before being chained in the bottomless pit for 1000 years, is accelerating his demonic forces to bring disaster, destruction, and danger into every human being's life. He is desperately seeking the souls of humanity before God brings an end to his rulership here on earth. Our world is accelerating towards its imminent destruction. Everyone is finding it difficult to live a normal life in this stress-filled world where lawlessness prevails, and violent crimes are a daily occurrence.

Jesus warned there would be perilous times in the last days before his coming. **Our generation is now witnessing all these End-Time signs.**

2 Timothy 3 KJV

> *1 This know also, that in the last days perilous times shall come.*

> *2 For men shall be lovers of their own selves, covetous, boasters, proud, blasphemers, disobedient to parents, unthankful, unholy,*

> *3 Without natural affection, trucebreakers, false accusers, incontinent, fierce, despisers of those that are good,*

4 Traitors, heady, highminded, lovers of pleasures more than lovers of God;

5 Having a form of godliness, but denying the power thereof: from such turn away.

6 For of this sort are they which creep into houses, and lead captive silly women laden with sins, led away with divers lusts,

7 Ever learning, and never able to come to the knowledge of the truth.

8 Now as Jannes and Jambres withstood Moses, so do these also resist the truth: men of corrupt minds, reprobate concerning the faith.

9 But they shall proceed no further: for their folly shall be manifest unto all men, as their's also was.

10 But thou hast fully known my doctrine, manner of life, purpose, faith, longsuffering, charity, patience,

11 Persecutions, afflictions, which came unto me at Antioch, at Iconium, at Lystra; what persecutions I endured: but out of them all the Lord delivered me.

12 Yea, and all that will live godly in Christ Jesus shall suffer persecution.

13 But evil men and seducers shall wax worse and worse, deceiving, and being deceived.

14 But continue thou in the things which thou hast learned and hast been assured of, knowing of whom thou hast learned them;

15 And that from a child thou hast known the holy scriptures, which are able to make thee wise unto salvation through faith which is in Christ Jesus.

16 All scripture is given by inspiration of God, and is profitable for doctrine, for reproof, for correction, for instruction in righteousness:

17 That the man of God may be perfect, thoroughly furnished unto all good works.

Political unrest and corruption are prevalent in our world governments today. Moral values do not line up with God's Ten

Commandments. There's a threat of financial bankruptcy, which is plaguing our country with no financial recovery in sight. Our world has never seen or experienced such cataclysmic events that are increasing at such accelerated speed. Never in man's entire recorded history have all these prophetic signs happened at the same time in one generation. The Bible gives an amazing amount of wisdom and inspirational solutions on how to cope with these real-life trials that affect us all personally, professionally, and spiritually. We all have an incredible wealth of knowledge by applying God's wise biblical counsel in making life-altering decisions to survive through these problematic times, and turn our trials into triumphs. Not only is the Bible riveting, inspiring, and educational, but it offers divine counsel from God's own words, in making the most important decision in one's life, and that is, where will we spend eternity when we die? The only two options given to us from the Word of God are heaven or hell. From birth, everyone was given "free will.". The Bible promises if we love God, repent of our sins, make Jesus our lord and savior, and comply with His laws, we go to heaven. If we serve Satan, and follow him, we go straight to the eternal fires in hell.

After Satan beguiled Adam and Eve into disobeying God and committing their first sin in the Garden of Eden, God made a way for them and their seed to be set free from His judgment of death. God offered His only son, Jesus, as the perfect sacrifice and atonement for mankind's sins, past, present, and future. By dying on the cross, Jesus willingly took upon Himself our sins and punishment and gave us His righteousness in exchange. All we need to do is repent of our sins and accept Jesus as our Lord and Savior. If we refuse God's grace of salvation through His son, Jesus, and follow the devil, we will spend eternity in the fires of hell.

This book includes the prophetic signs and wonders of these final days, with scriptures from both the Old and New Testaments, God's creation of Adam and Eve 6000 years ago, the trinity of God, salvation through our Lord and Savior Jesus Christ, the Holy Spirit, and His nine spiritual gifts, and God's adversary, Satan, the devil. **This book is divinely inspired, and a must-read for all who seek wise biblical counsel for this life and to have eternal salvation through Christ in God's earthly kingdom.**

Chapter 1
VIRGINIA FINDS HER DECEASED DAUGHTER'S GOD-INSPIRED MANUSCRIPT

On November 25, 2013, Virginia's daughter, Patty Lynne, at the age of 54, was taken home to be with the Lord. Her autopsy revealed she had stage four ovarian cancer. Since childhood, she chose to make the right decision to repent of her sins and accept Jesus Christ as her Lord and Savior. She diligently read and studied the Bible throughout her young and adult life. Patty Lynne's incredible discernment of life's issues was solely gleaned from her countless years of reading and studying the Word of God. She was gifted with answers on how to get through many of life's issues, which we all face while living in this satanically inspired world filled with confusion and upheavals.

After the passing of Virginia's family, and the tragedy that struck her life with her only son, she felt inspired to write this third book. She found Patty Lynne's manuscript with the card on top of her manuscript that read: *"This is what the Lord, the God of Israel says: 'write in a book all the words I have spoken to you'"* (Jeremiah 30:2 NIV).

This gave birth to Virginia's third God-inspired book, " *Virginia O'Hare Declares God's Final Warning to the World."*

1

Chapter 2
PATTY LYNNE'S MANUSCRIPT DESCRIBES GOD'S SIX DAYS OF CREATION

On the first day, the Lord God re-created the heavens and the earth and light from this dark void-less planet. (see Genesis 1:1-5). The heavens were everything beyond the earth's outer space. After God spoke all things into existence, something strange and wonderful began to happen. Silently, mysteriously, the heavy moisture-laden mist begins to rise.

All night and all the next morning, it went up, up, up, until it became a beautiful fluffy-white covering high above the earth, and water is present. There is clear fresh air forming the "atmosphere." *"Then God said, 'Let there be a firmament in the midst of the waters, and let it divide the waters from the waters.' Thus God made the firmament and divided the waters which were under the firmament from the waters which were above the firmament, and it was so. And God called the firmament Heaven. So the evening and the morning were **the second day**"* (Genesis 1:6-8 NKJV).

On the third day, God created the dry land with continents and islands above the water. The large bodies of water are named "seas," and the ground is named "land." God declared that all this is good. *"Then God said, 'Let the waters under the heavens be gathered together into one place, and let the dry land appear'; and it was so. And God called the dry land Earth, and the gathering together of the waters He called Seas. And God saw that it was good. Then God said, 'Let the earth bring forth grass, the herb that yields seed, and the fruit tree that yields fruit according to its kind, whose seed is in itself, on the earth'; and it was so. And the earth brought forth grass, the herb that yields seed according to its kind, and the tree that yields fruit, whose seed is in itself according to its kind. And God saw that it was good"* (Genesis 1:9-12 NKJV).

There is a mighty shaking and shuttering as out of its depths rises the first appearance of land. Swiftly, continents and islands begin to take shape. Mountains and hills move upward, as water drains from their sides in foaming cataracts. Out of a seemingly great earthquake, this land has mysteriously risen out of the ocean in all shapes and sizes. They made their glorious appearance. They are covered with grass, bushes, trees, tall glorious pines, cedars, redwoods, reaching clear to the top of the highest peaks. The fields were beauty masses of flowers of all colors blanketing the earth. God took great pleasure, making them all different from the others and giving every one of them the power to reproduce after its kind throughout all time to come. God took special interest making the fruit trees, plum, apple, pear, orange, lemon, avocado, with each one reproducing after its own fruit. For God was not thinking of himself when restoring this planet, but of someone who only existed in His mind, who would soon be a real living being in His likeness and image. He was planning to give all the beauty, and all this wealth of treasures and delight to someone He had not yet created. He added all the gold, silver, and precious stones that sparkled and glistened amid the grass and flowers, with all the provisions of nuts, fruits, and grains. **What a night! What a day!**

Now dawn begins to break from the bright cloud above the firmament. *"Then God said, 'Let there be lights in the firmament of the heavens to divide the day from the night; and let them be for signs and seasons, and for days and years; and let them be for lights in the firmament of the heavens to give light on the earth'; and it was so. Then God made two great lights: the greater light to rule the day and the lesser light to rule the night. He made the stars also. God set them in the firmament of the heavens to give light on the earth, and to rule over the day and over the night, and to divide the light from the darkness. And God saw that it was good. So the evening and the morning were* **the fourth day**" (Genesis 1:14-19 NKJV).

On the fifth day, God creates all life that lives in the water. Any life of any kind that lives in the water is made at this point. God also makes all the birds. All these creatures are made with the ability to perpetuate their species by reproduction. The creatures made on day five are the first creatures blessed by God. Prior to this, there wasn't a sound to be heard. *"Then God said, 'Let the waters abound with an abundance of living creatures, and let birds fly above the earth across the face of the firmament of the heavens.' So God created great sea creatures and every living thing that moves, with which the waters abounded, according to their kind, and every winged bird according to its kind. And God saw that it was good. And God blessed them, saying, 'Be fruitful and multiply, and fill the waters in the seas, and let birds multiply on the earth'"* (Genesis 1:20-22 NKJV).

Now God made the animals and the living creatures. Before God created man, He took counsel with His Son Jesus and His Holy Spirit and said, *"Let Us make man in Our image, according to Our likeness; let them have dominion over the fish of the sea, over the birds of the air, and over the cattle, over all the earth and over every creeping thing that creeps on the earth."* (Genesis 1:26 NKJV). God made man special above all the other creatures and even his angels and placed man in authority over the earth and over all the other creatures.

*"So God created man in His own image; in the image of God, He created him; male and female He created them. Then God blessed them, and God said to them, 'Be fruitful and multiply; fill the earth and subdue it; have dominion over the fish of the sea, over the birds of the air, and over every living thing that moves on the earth.' And God said, 'See, I have given you every herb that yields seed which is on the face of all the earth, and every tree whose fruit yields seed; to you it shall be for food. Also, to every beast of the earth, to every bird of the air, and to everything that creeps on the earth, in which there is life, I have given every green herb for food'; and it was so. Then God saw everything that He had made, and indeed it was very good. So the evening and the morning were **the sixth day**"* (Genesis 1:27-31 NKJV).

God's work was now complete. The entire universe in all its beauty and perfection was fully formed in six days, and God announced that it is very good.

On **the seventh day**, God rested from all his works and blessed and sanctified this day as a holy day. *"Thus the heavens and the earth, and all the host of them, were finished. And on the seventh day God ended His work which He had done, and He rested on the seventh day from all His work which He had done. Then God blessed the seventh day and sanctified it, because in it He rested from all His work which God had created and made"* (Genesis 2:1-3 NKJV).

The keeping of this seventh day will be kept by god's chosen people. *"Remember the Sabbath day by keeping it holy. Six days you shall labor and do all your work, but the seventh day is a sabbath to the Lord your God. On it you shall not do any work, neither you, nor your son or daughter, nor your male or female servant, nor your animals, nor any foreigner residing in your towns. For in six days the Lord made the heavens and the earth, the sea, and all that is in them, but he rested on the seventh day. Therefore the Lord blessed the Sabbath day and made it holy"* (Exodus 20:8-11 NIV).

According to God's timetable, His six days of creation equates to six thousand years. The Bible documents that one day to the Lord is 1000 years. *"But, beloved, be not ignorant of this one thing, that one day is with the Lord as a thousand years, and a thousand years as one day"* (2 Peter 3:8 KJV).

Chapter 3
CRUCIFIXION OF JESUS CHRIST REDEEMED US FROM THE CURSE OF THE LAW
GENESIS 3:15

God created angels before he created time, space, energy, and mankind. He created our universe out of matter and the power of His spoken Word through His only Beloved Son, Jesus Christ. Before God laid out the foundations of the universe, it was dark and void. Upon seeing the wondrous works of God being created before their eyes, all the angels shouted for joy (Job 38:4-7).

Angelic beings were given status positions. Seraphims ranked in the highest angelic class. They serve as the caretakers of God's throne and continuously shout praises: "Holy, holy, holy is the Lord of hosts; the whole earth is full of His glory!" Isaiah 6:1–7 NKJV Angels are servants of God and minister to all believers (Hebrews 1:4).

Arch Angel Lucifer, also known as the light bearing one, had the highest-ranking position, and was the most beautiful angel God created. His beauty was beyond description. He was perfect in wisdom, a musician who held an exalted position of hovering over the very throne of God and a leader of angels. From the beginning, he was good until pride, vanity, and jealousy of God's majesty became his obsession. (Ezekiel 28:15) He wanted to ascend above the stars of God, and receive all the praise and worship from the angels. He said, *"I will ascend into heaven, I will exalt my throne above the stars of God: I will sit also upon the mount of the congregation, in the sides of the north: I will ascend above the heights of the clouds; I will be like the most High"* (Isaiah 14:13-14 KJV).

Lucifer set in his mind to be like the most high. This is the first wrong thought he or anyone can have, to think they can be like or above God in any form, shape, or matter. Lucifer erroneously thought he could take full control and possess everything God created. To implement his faulty plan, he convinced a third of God's angels to join him in his rebellion against God, which was a complete failure. His intentional and defiant act of rebellion has caused our world such pain, chaos, and major turmoil.

After Satan and a third of the angels committed the unpardonable sin of rebelling against God, they were all cast out of heaven down to earth by the most powerful leader of God's army, Archangel Michael, and his angels. *"And the great dragon was cast out, that old serpent, called the Devil, and Satan, which deceiveth the whole world: he was cast out into the earth, and his angels were cast out with him"* (Revelation 12:9 KJV).

After Lucifer's fall, his name was changed to Satan, meaning God's adversary. The fallen angels were called demons. Satan's other diabolical names mentioned throughout the Bible are the devil, the dragon, serpent, tempter, and the father of lies. Satan seduces humans into thinking we can be independent of our creator. He used that same lie on the fallen angels as well as Adam and Eve. The truth is, no one can survive without God. We must align our mindset to this fact. Our eternal salvation depends on our knowing this. We must align ourselves to God, his laws, and keep our minds open to His Word. This is why the Holy Spirit inspired 40 men to write God's Words in the Bible, the oldest and best-selling book in the entire world. The Bible is our menu to peace, joy, happiness, and eternal salvation through Jesus.

God's creations are endless. We may never know all the answers to our questions until we get to heaven. One question the Bible is silent about is how many angels or stars did God create? The book of Daniel describes the number of angels as a myriad of myriads. This equates to 10,000 x 10,000, which is 100 million angelic beings. (see Daniel 7:10). There are 100 billion galaxies in the observable universe, with the number of stars varying in each galaxy. Assuming an average of 100 billion stars per galaxy would equate to about one billion trillion or 1,000,000,000,000,000,000,000 stars in the observable universe. Only God knows for sure how many stars are in the non-observable universe. *"He counts the number of the stars; He calls them all by name"* (Psalm 147:4 NKJV). Jesus said God counts the very number of hairs on our head. *"But the very hairs of your head are all numbered"* (Matthew 10:30 NKJV).There is no one who can compare to our almighty and powerful God.

Satan thought he could with his demons, who followed him in his rebellion against God in the first and only cosmic warfare in heaven. One of Satan's devious plans was to control the planet earth that God created for Adam and Eve. He knew of God's command to Adam, **not to eat the fruit from the Tree of Knowledge of Good and Evil,** or he would die. Satan wanted Adam to disobey God's commandment and die so he could take control of the earth. To achieve his goal, he turned himself into a talking serpent and appeared to Eve.

"He said to the woman, 'Did God really say, 'You must not eat from any tree in the garden?' The woman said to the serpent, 'We may eat fruit from the trees in the garden, but God did say, 'You must not eat fruit from the tree that is in the middle of the garden, and you must not touch it, or you will die.' 'You will not certainly die,' the serpent said to the woman. 'For God knows that when you eat from it your eyes will be opened, and you will be like God, knowing good and evil.' When the woman saw that the fruit of the tree was good for food and pleasing to the eye, and also desirable for gaining wisdom, she took some and ate it. She also gave some to her husband, who was with her, and he ate it. Then the eyes of both of them were opened, and they realized they were naked; so they sewed fig leaves together and made coverings for themselves. Then the man and his wife heard the sound of the Lord God as he was walking in the garden in the cool of the day, and they hid from the Lord God among the trees of the garden. But the Lord God called to the man, 'Where are you?' He answered, 'I heard you in the garden, and I was afraid because I was naked; so I hid.' And He said, 'Who told you that you were naked? Have you eaten from the tree that I commanded you not to eat from?' The man said, 'The woman you put here with me—she gave me some fruit from the tree, and I ate it.' Then the Lord God said to the woman, 'What is this you have done?' The woman said, 'The serpent deceived me, and I ate.'

So the Lord God said to the serpent, 'Because you have done this, Cursed are you above all livestock and all wild animals! You will crawl on your belly and you will eat dust all the days of your life. And I will put enmity between you and the woman, and between your offspring and hers; he will crush your head, and you will strike his heel.'

To the woman He said, 'I will make your pains in childbearing very severe; with painful labor you will give birth to children. Your desire will be for your husband, and he will rule over you.'

To Adam He said, 'Because you listened to your wife and ate fruit from the tree about which I commanded you, 'You must not eat from it,' Cursed is the ground because of you; through painful toil you will eat food from it all the days of your life. It will produce thorns and thistles for you, and you will eat the plants of the field. By the sweat of your brow you will eat your food until you return to the ground, since from it you were taken; for dust you are and to dust you will return'" (Genesis 3:1-19 NIV).

"The Lord God made garments of skin for Adam and his wife and clothed them. And the Lord God said, 'The man has now become like one of us, knowing good and evil. IIe must not be allowed to reach out his hand and take also from the tree of life and eat, and live forever.' So the Lord God banished him from the Garden of Eden to work the ground from which he had been taken. After He drove the man out, He placed on the east side of the Garden of Eden cherubim and a flaming sword flashing back and forth to guard the way to the tree of life" (Genesis 3:21-24 NIV).God was speaking here to Jesus and the Holy Spirit.

God placed his judgment on Satan, stating, *"I will put enmity between you and the woman, and between your offspring and hers; He [Jesus] will crush your head, and you [Satan] will strike his heel"* (Genesis 3:15 NIV).

The woman's seed, Jesus, did crush the head of Satan when He died on the Cross of Calvary, two thousand years ago, for man's sins. Upon His Second Coming, He will put an end to Satan's rulership of planet earth, sin, corruption, and death forever. He will set up His righteous kingdom here on earth, where He will be the Lord of Lords and King of Kings. He will rule the chosen and faithful with a righteous and incorruptible government that will last forever, *"So when this corruptible has put on incorruption, and this mortal has put on immortality, then shall be brought to pass the saying that is written: 'Death is swallowed up in victory'"* (1 Corinthians 15:54 NKJV).

God offers His amazing saving grace of salvation to humanity through his Son, our Savior, Jesus, as atonement for all their sins, past, present, and future. To attain this, Jesus had to be born of a virgin, live a perfect life, and die in our stead as punishment for the sins of the world. It was at that very moment, when Jesus died on the cross, two thousand years ago, that Satan, who brought sin and death into the Garden of Eden, was defeated. His fate was sealed forever by Jesus' death on the cross. Jesus paid the price in full for all of humanity's sins. Although the battle still rages in the world today, the outcome of the war between God and Satan has been determined. God wins, Satan loses, the angels win, and demons lose.

Unfortunately, from the beginning, Adam and Eve made wrong decisions that not only affected their lives but the lives of their offspring as well. Eve, the mother of all creation, used her free will to make a bad decision. She allowed a fallen angel to deceive her. We must comply with the laws of the One who created us, or we, like Adam, Eve, and Lucifer, will receive their judgment.

God, our Heavenly Father, will restore everything back to what it was before sin and death entered the world. Know that, as we go through the battle of warfare in our own life, God will always be present to give His mighty, powerful warrior angels charge over his saints and keep them in all their ways. **All we need to do is submit our life to God totally until there is nothing left for the devil to touch!** *"For He shall give His angels charge over you, To keep you in all your ways"* (Psalm 91:11 NKJV). One day soon, with the Second Coming of Jesus, God will restore everything as intended it to be from the beginning, and the world will be forever free from Satan, sin, and death.

Every believer has the Blessed Hope of God's promise of protection against the wiles of Satan, his demons, and all our earthly enemies. Without exception, anyone who comes against us in this life is defeated by God. He promises, *"'No weapon formed against you shall prosper, and every tongue which rises against you in judgment, you shall condemn. This is the heritage of the servants of the Lord, and their righteousness is from Me' says the Lord"* **(Isaiah 54:17 NKJV).**

Chapter 4
WHY DID JESUS COME TO EARTH?

TO BRING LIGHT TO A DARK WORLD

"I have come into the world as light so that whoever believes in Me may not remain in darkness" (John 12:46 NIV).

"By Him all things were created, both in the heavens and on earth, visible and invisible, whether thrones or dominions or rulers or authorities–all things have been created by Him and for Him" (Colossians 1:16 NASB).

"All things came into being by Him, and apart from Him, nothing came into being that has come into being" (John 1:3 NASB).

TO BE MADE LIKE HIS PEOPLE WHO HE CREATED

"Since therefore the children share in flesh and blood, He himself likewise partook of the same things, that through death He might destroy the one who has the power of death, that is, the devil, and deliver all those who through fear of death were subject to lifelong slavery. For surely it is not angels that He helps, but He helps the offspring of Abraham. Therefore, He had to be made like His brothers in every respect, so that He might become a merciful and faithful high priest in the service of God, to make propitiation for the sins of the people" (Hebrews 2:14-17 ESV).

TO BEAR WITNESS TO THE TRUTH

"Then Pilate said to Him, 'So you are a king?' Jesus answered, 'You say that I am a king. For this purpose, I was born, and for this purpose I have come into the world—to bear witness to the truth. Everyone who is of the truth listens to My voice'" (John 18:37 ESV).

TO DESTROY THE DEVIL AND HIS WORKS

"Since therefore the children share in flesh and blood, He himself likewise partook of the same things, that through death He might destroy the one who has the power of death, that is, the devil" (Hebrews 2:14 ESV).

"Whoever makes a practice of sinning is of the devil, for the devil has been sinning from the beginning. The reason the Son of God appeared was to destroy the works of the devil" (1 John 3:8 ESV).

TO GIVE ETERNAL LIFE

"I am the living bread that came down from heaven. If anyone eats of this bread, he will live forever. And the bread that I will give for the life of the world is My flesh" (John 6:51 ESV).

TO RECEIVE WORSHIP

"Now after Jesus was born in Bethlehem of Judea in the days of Herod, the king, behold, wise men from the east came to Jerusalem, saying, 'Where is He who has been born king of the Jews? For we saw His star when it rose and have come to worship him.' And going into the house they saw the Child with Mary, his mother, and they fell down and worshiped Him. Then, opening their treasures, they offered him gifts, gold and frankincense, and myrrh" (Matthew 2:1-2 ESV).

TO BRING GREAT JOY

"And the angel said to them, 'Fear not, for behold, I bring you Good News of great joy that will be for all the people'" (Luke 2:10 ESV).

TO DEMONSTRATE TRUE HUMILITY

"Have this mind among yourselves, which is yours in Christ Jesus, who, though He was in the form of God, did not count equality with God a thing to be grasped, but emptied Himself, by taking the form of a servant, being born in the likeness of men. And being found in human form, He humbled himself by becoming obedient to the point of death, even death on a cross" (Philippians 2:5-8 ESV).

TO PREACH THE GOSPEL OF THE KINGDOM OF GOD

"The spirit of the Lord is upon me because He has anointed me to proclaim Good News to the poor. He has sent me to proclaim liberty to the captives and recovering of sight to the blind, to set at liberty those who are oppressed, to proclaim the year of the Lord's favor…but he said to them, "I must preach the Good News of the Kingdom of God to the other towns as well; for I was sent for this purpose" (Luke 4:18-19 ESV).

TO BRING JUDGMENT

"Jesus said, 'For judgment I came into this world, that those who do not see may see, and those who see may become blind.' Some of the Pharisees near Him heard these things and said to Him, 'Are we also blind?' Jesus said to them, 'If you were blind, you would have no guilt; but now that you say, 'we see,' your guilt remains'" (John 9:39-41 ESV).

TO GIVE HIS LIFE AS A RANSOM FOR MANY

"For even the Son of Man came not to be served but to serve, and to give His life as a ransom for many" (Mark 10:45 ESV).

"…waiting for our Blessed Hope, the appearing of the Glory of our great God and Savior Jesus Christ, who gave Himself for us to redeem us from all lawlessness and to purify for Himself a people for His own possession who are zealous for good works" (Titus 2:13-14 ESV).

TO FULFILL THE LAW AND PROPHETS

"For truly, I say to you, until heaven and earth pass away, not an iota, not a dot, will pass from the law until all is accomplished" (Matthew 5:17 ESV).

TO REVEAL GOD'S LOVE FOR SINNERS

"For God so loved the world, that He gave His only son, that whoever believes in Him should not perish but have eternal life." (John 3:16 ESV).

TO CALL SINNERS TO REPENTANCE

"And when Jesus heard it, He said to them, 'Those who are well have no need of a physician, but those who are sick. I came not to call the righteous, but sinners'" (Mark 2:17 ESV).

TO DIE FOR ALL SINNERS AND TAKE ON HIMSELF THEIR PUNISHMENT

"Truly, truly, I say to you, unless a grain of wheat falls into the earth and dies, it remains alone; but if it dies, it bears much fruit. Whoever loves his life loses it, and whoever hates his life in this world will keep it for eternal life. If anyone serves Me, he must

follow Me; and where I am, there will my servant be also. If anyone serves Me, the Father will honor him. Now is my soul troubled. And what shall I say? 'Father, save me from this hour?' But for this purpose, I have come to this hour" (John 12:24-27 ESV).

TO SEEK AND SAVE THE LOST

"And when Jesus came to the place, He looked up and said to him, 'Zacchaeus, hurry and come down, for I must stay at your house today.' And Jesus said to him, 'Today salvation has come to this house since he also is a son of Abraham. For the Son of Man came to seek and to save the lost'" (Luke 19:5 ESV).

TO SERVE MANKIND AND BE A RANSOM FOR MANY

"For even the Son of Man came not to be served but to serve, and to give His life as a ransom for many" (Mark 10:45 ESV).

TO BRING PEACE AND SET MAN FREE FROM SIN AND DEATH

"For He Himself is our peace, who has made us both one and has broken down in His flesh the dividing wall of hostility by 'abolishing the law of commandments expressed in ordinances, that He might create in Himself one new man in place of the two, so making peace, and might reconcile us both to God in one body through the cross, thereby killing the hostility. And He came and preached peace to you who were far off and peace to those who were near. For through Him we both have access in one spirit to the father" (Ephesians 2:14-18 ESV).

"For sin will have no dominion over you, since you are not under law but under grace" (Romans 6:14 ESV).

"There is therefore now no condemnation for those who are in Christ Jesus. For the law of the Spirit of life has set you free in Christ Jesus from the law of sin and death" (Romans 8:1-2 ESV).

TO BRING A SWORD, AND TO BE FIRST IN OUR LIFE OVER ANYONE ELSE

"Do not suppose that I have come to bring peace to the earth. I did not come to bring peace, but a sword. For I have come to turn a man against his father, a daughter against her mother, a daughter-in-law against her mother-in-law— a man's enemies will be the members of his own household. Anyone who loves their father or mother more than Me is not worthy of Me; anyone who loves their son or daughter more than Me is not worthy of Me. Whoever does not take up their cross and follow Me is not worthy of Me. Whoever finds their life will lose it, and whoever loses their life for My sake will find it" (Matthew 10:34-39 NIV).

TO BIND UP BROKEN HEARTS

"The spirit of the Lord God is upon me, because the Lord has anointed me to bring good news to the poor; he has sent me to bind up the brokenhearted, to proclaim liberty to the captives, and the opening of the prison to those who are bound; to proclaim the year of the Lord's favor, and the day of vengeance of our God; to comfort all who mourn; to grant to those who mourn in Zion— to give them a beautiful headdress instead of ashes, the oil of gladness instead of mourning, the garment of praise instead of a faint spirit; that they may be called oaks of righteousness, the planting of the Lord, that He may be glorified" (Isaiah 61:1-3 ESV).

TO GIVE US THE HOLY SPIRIT

"And I will ask the Father, and he will give you another helper, (the Holy Spirit) to be with you forever, even the spirit of truth,

whom the world cannot receive, because it neither sees Him nor knows Him. You know Him, for he dwells with you and will be in you" (John 14:16-17 ESV).

TO MAKE US PARTAKERS OF THE DIVINE NATURE

"...by which He has granted to us His precious and very great promises, so that through them you may become partakers of the divine nature, having escaped from the corruption that is in the world because of sinful desire" (2 Peter 1:4 ESV).

TO REIGN AS THE KING OF KINGS AND LORD OF LORDS

"For to us a child is born, to us a Son is given; and the government shall be upon His shoulder, and his name shall be called Wonderful Counselor, Mighty God, Everlasting Father, Prince of Peace. Of the increase of His government and of peace there will be no end, on the throne of David and over His kingdom, to establish it and to uphold it with justice and with righteousness from this time forth and forevermore. The zeal of the Lord of Hosts will do this" (Isaiah 9:6-7 ESV).

TO RESTORE HUMAN NATURE TO HOLINESS

"And the angel answered her, 'The Holy Spirit will come upon you, and the power of the most high will overshadow you; therefore, the child to be born will be called Holy—the Son of God" (Luke 1:35 ESV).

TO BE A MERCIFUL AND FAITHFUL HIGH PRIEST IN THE SERVICE OF GOD

"Therefore, He had to be made like his brothers in every respect, so that He might become a merciful and faithful high priest in the service of God, to make propitiation for the sins of the people. For

because He himself has suffered when tempted, He is able to help those who are being tempted" (Hebrews 2:17-18 ESV).

TO BE THE SECOND ADAM AND ATONE FOR THE FIRST ADAM'S SIN AND DEATH

"Yet death reigned from Adam to Moses, even over those whose sinning was not like the transgression of Adam, who was a type of the one who was to come. But the free gift is not like the trespass. For if many died through one man's trespass, much more have the grace of God and the free gift by the grace of that one man Jesus Christ abounded for many" (Romans 5:14-15 ESV).

TO SATISFY MAN'S DEEPEST THIRST FOR ETERNAL LIFE

"Jesus said to her, 'Everyone who drinks of this water will be thirsty again, but whoever drinks of the water that I will give him will never be thirsty again. The water that I will give him will become in him a spring of water welling up to eternal life'" (John 4:13-14 ESV).

TO BE SENT BY GOD TO SAVE HUMANITY

"Jesus said to them, 'If God were your father, you would love Me, for I came from God and I am here. I came not of My own accord, but He sent me'" (John 8:42 ESV).

TO REVEAL GOD'S GLORY, GRACE, AND TRUTH

"And the Word became flesh and dwelt among us, and we have seen His glory, glory as of the only Son from the Father, full of grace and truth" (John 1:1 ESV).

To accomplish His assignment to save humanity from their sins, Jesus had to make a decision, which was to obey the will of His Father and proclaim His gospel of salvation to the world. To do this, He had to be willing to give His life as atonement for the sins of the world and bear all the just punishments that we as sinners deserve. He willingly took our chastisement for every sin we ever committed, past, present, and future with his crucifixion on the cross. Now, all we have to do to be saved is to repent of our sins and accept the sacrifice Jesus made for us with His life. Then, we can live forever in God's heavenly kingdom here on earth. If one makes the wrong decision and rejects God's free gift of salvation through His only begotten son Jesus Christ, that person will spend an eternity in the fires of hell, where Satan and the fallen angels will join the false prophet and the anti-christ forever.

Not only was everything created by and for Jesus, nothing was made without him, that was made. He gave His life, so we, who He created, could be free of our sins and our sinful nature and not have to go to hell. *"In the past God spoke to our ancestors through the prophets at many times and in various ways, but in these last days he has spoken to us by his Son, whom he appointed heir of all things, and through whom also he made the universe. The Son is the radiance of God's glory and the exact representation of his being, sustaining all things by his powerful word. After He had provided purification for sins, He sat down at the right hand of the Majesty in heaven. So He became as much superior to the angels as the name He has inherited is superior to theirs"* (Hebrews 1:1-4 NIV).

Prior to the final battle of Armageddon, Jesus will rapture all those who have fallen asleep and repented of their sins and accepted Jesus as their Lord and Savior. Then those who are alive, who repented of their sins and accepted him as their Lord and Savior, will also be taken together with them into heaven. What a reunion that will be, to be reunited with all our saved loved ones. But those who reject God's offer of salvation through His Son, Jesus, will be damned forever. The Bible makes it abundantly clear, Satan and all those who oppose God will be defeated in the final battle of Armageddon, where Jesus will defeat Satan and all those nations who come against God. Then a mighty angel will not only chain Satan but cast him into the bottomless pit for 1000 years while the redeemed in Christ will dwell during the millennium, in peace, joy, and happiness! *"And I saw an angel coming down out of heaven, having the key to the Abyss and holding in his hand a great chain. He seized the dragon, that ancient serpent, who is the devil, or Satan, and bound him for a thousand years. He threw him into the Abyss, and locked and sealed it over him, to keep him from deceiving the nations anymore until the thousand years were ended. After that, he must be set free for a short time"* (Revelation 20:1-3 NIV).

Since his fall, Satan seeks revenge against God and humanity. He is both God's adversary and man's worst enemy. His evil wiles are perpetual and never-ending. There is no love or good found in him or his demons. They use their power to infiltrate our minds and hearts with only evil and lustful thoughts and desires. Satan's battlefield, and his first line of attack, is in our minds. We must guard our conscious and subconscious thoughts because he tries to cause everyone to stray from God and his commandments. He did this with Adam and Eve and will continue his attacks on everyone until Jesus returns. In the meantime, we must safeguard our minds and not allow Satan to impregnate us with his evil thoughts and destructive desires. To avoid this, it is essential that we align ourselves with God's precepts, which blocks Satan's attacks and keep him at bay. *"Do not conform to the pattern of this world, but be transformed by the renewing of your mind. Then you will be able to test and approve what God's will is—his good, pleasing and perfect will"* (Romans 12:2 NIV).

Chapter 5
CHRIST WILL REIGN FOREVER

Revelation 11:15 ESV

"Then the seventh angel sounded; and there were loud voices in heaven, saying, 'the kingdom of the world has become the kingdom of our Lord and of his Christ; and he will reign forever and ever.'"

1 Kings 2:33 ESV

"So shall their blood return on the head of Joab and on the head of his descendants forever; but to David and his descendants and his house and his throne, may there be peace from the Lord forever."

1 Kings 2:45 ESV

"But King Solomon shall be blessed, and the throne of David shall be established before the Lord forever."

Psalm 89:29 NASB

"So, I will establish his descendants forever and his throne as the days of heaven."

Psalm 89:36 KJ21

"His Seed shall endure forever and His throne as the sun before me."

Psalm 89:37 KJV

"It shall be established forever like the moon, and the witness in the sky is faithful."

Psalm 132:12 NKJV

"If your sons will keep My covenant and My testimony which I will teach them, their sons also shall sit upon your throne forever."

Ezekiel 37:25 NASB

"They will live on the land that I gave to Jacob My servant, in which your fathers lived; and they will live on it, they, and their sons and their sons' sons, forever; and David My servant will be their prince forever. "

2 Samuel 7:13 ESV

"He shall build a house for My name, and I will establish the throne of his kingdom forever."

2 Samuel 7:16 NASB

"Your house and your kingdom shall endure before Me forever; your throne shall be established forever."

1 Chronicles 22:10 ESV

"He shall build a house for My name, and he shall be My son and I will be his father; and I will establish the throne of his kingdom over Israel forever."

1 Chronicles 28:7 NASB

"I will establish his kingdom forever if he resolutely performs My commandments and my ordinances, as is done now."

Psalm 45:6 ESV

"Your throne, O God, is forever and ever; a scepter of uprightness is the scepter of Your kingdom."

Hebrews 1:8 NASB

But of the Son He says, "Your throne, O God, is forever and ever, and the righteous scepter is the scepter of His kingdom."

Daniel 7:14 ESV

"And to Him was given dominion, glory and a kingdom, that all the peoples, nations and men of every language might serve Him; His dominion is an everlasting dominion which will not pass away; And His kingdom is one which will not be destroyed."

Luke 1:33 ESV

"And He will reign over the house of Jacob forever, and of His kingdom there will be no end."

Daniel 2:44 NASB

"In the days of those kings the God of heaven will set up a kingdom which will never be destroyed, and that kingdom will not be left for another people; it will crush and put an end to all these kingdoms, but it will itself endure forever."

2 Peter 1:11 NASB

"For in this way, the entrance into the eternal kingdom of our Lord and Savior Jesus Christ will be abundantly supplied to you."

Revelation 1:6 ESV

"He has made us to be a kingdom, priests to His God and Father- -to Him be the glory and the dominion forever and ever." Amen

Chapter 6
SATAN'S TEMPTATIONS

Scripture warns that anyone who delves into any satanic activities will not inherit the kingdom of God. Instead, we must all keep feeding our free will with self-control and doing the will of God. Then, Satan's fire, that comes to destroy us, is instantly put out.

Satan's temptations include: Sexual immorality, impurity, idolatry, sorcery, enmity, strife, jealousy, fits of anger, rivalries, dissensions, envy, drunkenness, orgies, deep depression, obstinacy, indiscretion, a restless spirit, pride, vanity, despair, discouragement, uncontrollable anger, disobedience, hardness of heart, stubborn resentment, uncontrolled anger, strong inclination to sensuality, and hypocrisy.

When we resist the devil, we cut off his fuel source. Then his evil temptations and burning fire are totally quenched. The life span of thoughts is determined by how much attention is given to it. A fire can only burn as long as you fuel it. A thought cannot exist without attention given to it; therefore, a negative thought is cut off when you give no attention to it. We must put our thoughts on positive things and not negative ones. We should use our time wisely in doing productive and useful things. The reason we get ourselves in trouble is that we forget the fact we were created for a higher purpose than to entertain the dark forces of sin in our life. We mess up when we are too busy wondering what others are doing and saying. This is meddling, which is unproductive. Let God show us our purpose even if things don't come to pass right away. **We must persevere in faith!** Our skills only develop when we learn to focus our ability, talents, and attention on what we were called to do, and that is to fulfill our destiny. We all have a purpose, but we sometimes hook up with people who stop us from fulfilling the goals that lead us to our destiny. We must strive forward and not be stationary or look back. Solomon, the wisest man who ever lived, wrote that the whole purpose of man is to fear God and keep His commandments. *"Let us hear the conclusion of the whole matter: Fear God, and keep his commandments: for this is the whole duty of man"* (Ecclesiastes 12:13 KJV).**Man's chief end is to glorify God and enjoy a relationship with him forever**.

SCRIPTURES TO OVERCOME SATANIC ATTACKS:

James 4:7 ESV

> *"Submit yourselves therefore to God. Resist the devil, and he will flee from you."*

1 Peter 5:8-9 ESV

> *"Be sober-minded; be watchful. Your adversary, the devil, prowls around like a roaring lion, seeking someone to devour. Resist him, firm in your faith, knowing that the same kinds of suffering are being experienced by your brotherhood throughout the world."*

2 Corinthians 4:4 ESV

> *"In their case the god of this world (Satan) has blinded the minds of the unbelievers, to keep them from seeing the light of the gospel of the glory of Christ, who is the image of God."*

Ephesians 6:11 ESV

"Put on the whole armor of God, that you may be able to stand against the schemes of the devil."

2 Corinthians 11:3 ESV

"But I am afraid that as the serpent deceived Eve by his cunning, your thoughts will be led astray from a sincere and pure devotion to Christ."

1 Corinthians 10:13 ESV

"No temptation has overtaken you that is not common to man. God is faithful, and He will not let you be tempted beyond your ability, but with the temptation He will also provide the way of escape, that you may be able to endure it."

Ephesians 4:27 ESV

"And give no opportunity to the devil."

Matthew 16:23 ESV

"But He turned and said to Peter, "get behind Me, Satan! You are a hindrance to Me. For you are not setting your mind on the things of God, but on the things of man."

Romans 8:5 ESV

"For those who live according to the flesh set their minds on the things of the flesh, but those who live according to the Spirit set their minds on the things of the Spirit."

2 Thessalonians 3:3 ESV

"But the Lord is faithful. He will establish you and guard you against the evil one."

1 Corinthians 6:19-20 ESV

"Or do you not know that your body is a temple of the Holy Spirit within you, whom you have from God? You are not your own, for you were bought with a price. So, glorify God in your body."

Luke 10:19 ESV

"Behold, I have given you authority to tread on serpents and scorpions, and over all the power of the enemy, and nothing shall hurt you."

Chapter 7
CHOOSE ONLY POSITIVE THOUGHTS TO ENTER YOUR MIND

Find something to do that's in your heart that will make you proud. Then, something will happen, and you will know you are on the right path to success. The battle is not ours; it belongs to God. Let Him handle all your problems and see His victory and triumphs, which He always provides. Be positive, watch your words, because every single conversation you listen to can affect your thinking and decisions. Be careful what you allow your ears to hear, your eyes to see, and the words you speak. This will determine what path you will take to fulfill your goals in this life. We should never lean on our own understanding but lean on God alone and not man. God knows all our needs. He sees everything and cares for us. He loves our trusting and leaning on Him for everything. God is our father! He wants to counsel and direct us always towards the right path. Let him guide you in making all your decisions; then, you will never go wrong. Keep your heart humble and sincere. Do not be conceited, narcissistic, or haughty minded. Having success in one's life is trusting in God and not in man or yourself. ***"Trust in the Lord with all thine heart; and lean not unto thine own understanding. In all thy ways acknowledge him, and he shall direct thy paths"*** (Proverbs 3:5-6 KJV).

When your obsession is doing the right thing, the wrong people in your life find you unbearable. The best way to disconnect from the wrong people is to become obsessed with doing only the right thing and ignoring their confrontational spirit. Every decision you make reveals your faith or your fears. Every gift within you is a necessity for your assignment. Your rightful goals allow your "true" friends to confirm their loyalty to you. Stop looking to where you have been and start looking at where you can be.

Every gift within you is a necessity for your assignment. If anyone believes in your gifts, that's good. If anyone does not because they are jealous of your future goals and success, immediately depart from such negativity and continue to go forward. Keep believing in yourself. Satan always attacks at the birth of something significant in your life. This could be your ministry or anything God directs you to accomplish. Your future success is knowing your assignment, which the Holy Spirit will qualify you to pursue. **It is impossible to please God without faith**. We must always trust in him. Your assignments in life allow the Holy Spirit to prepare you to obtain your goals. His presence and gifts are unending. **Never stay where you have not been assigned.**

A true warrior continues to live by a code of honor even when everyone around him is lying, cheating, and compromising their values to get ahead. A man of honor owns up to his mistakes. He stands tall, while others fall. The day will come when you have so much truth inside you, that many will follow your counsel and seek your advice. Never complain about what you permit in your life. Learn from your mistakes. Your significance is not in your similarities to another but in your differences. To be able to work out your differences with respect to one another, you must be understanding and patient. This is a virtue. Master God's gift of love, and you have mastered life completely. **Pain is not your enemy; it merely proves you are alive and can be healed.** Your success is decided by what you are willing to accomplish and not what you ignore and fail to do. Futility is merely a feeling, conquer it, and keep heading forward.

Miracles do happen in everyone's life! Embrace them, and thank God for them. A miracle can happen at any place, at any time. The size of the place does not matter to a miracle. Jesus' first miracle was at a wedding in Cana, a town in Galilee, where he turned water into wine. (see John 2:1-11).

Jesus creates miracles in every believer's life. All we have to do is ask, seek, and knock. *"Ask, and it shall be given you; seek, and ye shall find; knock, and it shall be opened unto you: For every one that asketh receiveth; and he that seeketh findeth; and to him that knocketh it shall be opened"* **(Matthew 7:7-8 KJV).**

THERE IS LIFE AND DEATH IN THE TONGUE

Words start our battles, and words end our battles. We must avoid perverse speech because there is life and death in the tongue, and what a man thinks he is. *"For as he thinks in his heart, so is he"* **(Proverbs 23:7 NKJV).** Whatsoever a man sows in this life; he shall also reap. *"Do not be deceived: God cannot be mocked. A man reaps what he sows. Whoever sows to please their flesh, from the flesh will reap destruction; whoever sows to please the Spirit, from the Spirit will reap eternal life. Let us not become weary in doing good, for at the proper time we will reap a harvest if we do not give up"* **(Galatians 6:7-9 NIV).**

One must carefully choose their words and what they say. The wise man restrains his tongue and the number of his words. *"The one who talks much will for sure sin, but he who is careful what he says is wise"* (Proverbs 10:19 NLV) Oftentimes, when we have said too much, we will realize that we would have been better off if we had said nothing at all. *"But I tell you that every careless word that people speak, they shall give an accounting for it in the day of judgment. For by your words you will be justified, and by your words you will be condemned"* (Matthew 12:36-37 NASB). **Everyone will give an account on judgment day for their actions and spoken words.**

SPEAK EDIFYING WORDS TO OTHERS

Ephesians 4:29 KJV

"Let no corrupt communication proceed out of your mouth, but that which is good to the use of edifying, that it may minister grace unto the hearers."

Psalms 141:3 KJV

"Set a watch, O Lord, before my mouth; keep the door of my lips."

Psalms 19:14 KJV

"Let the words of my mouth, and the meditation of my heart, be acceptable in Thy sight, O Lord, my strength, and my redeemer."

Psalms 49:3 KJV

"My mouth shall speak of wisdom; and the meditation of my heart shall be of understanding."

Proverbs 8:13 KJV

"The fear of the Lord is to hate evil: pride, and arrogancy, and the evil way, and the froward mouth, do I hate."

Proverbs 18:13 KJV

"He that answereth a matter before he heareth it, it is folly and shame unto him."

Proverbs 18:21 KJV

"Death and life [are] in the power of the tongue: and they that love it shall eat the fruit thereof."

James 1:19 KJV

"Wherefore, My beloved brethren, let every man be swift to hear, slow to speak, slow to wrath."

James 3:2-10 KJV

"For in many things we offend all. If any man offend not in word, the same [is] a perfect man, [and] able also to bridle the whole body."

James 3:9-10 KJV

"Therewith bless we God, even the Father; and therewith curse we men, which are made after the similitude of God."

Proverbs 15:1 KJV

"A soft answer turneth away wrath: but grievous words stir up anger."

Psalms 37:30-31 KJV

"The mouth of the righteous speaketh wisdom, and his tongue talketh of judgment."

Proverbs 16:24 KJV

"Pleasant words [are as] an honeycomb, sweet to the soul, and health to the bones."

Proverbs 21:23 KJV

"Whoso keepeth his mouth and his tongue keepeth his soul from troubles."

Colossians 3:17 KJV

"And whatsoever ye do in word or deed, do all in the name of the Lord Jesus, giving thanks to God and the Father by him."

Ephesians 4:15 KJV

"But speaking the truth in love, may grow up into him in all things, which is the head, even Christ."

Proverbs 15:4 KJV

"A wholesome tongue [is] a tree of life: but perverseness therein [is] a breach in the spirit."

James 5:12 KJV

"But above all things, my brethren, swear not, neither by heaven, neither by the earth, neither by any other oath: but let your yea be yea; and [your] nay, nay; lest ye fall into condemnation."

It is very easy to cause harm with thoughtless words and rude mannerisms; we need to closely monitor our words and our actions and not be offensive to others. Each moment of our life is an opportunity we have to be loving, kind, and thoughtful towards one another. We must also keep our eyes on only good and edifying things that will bless our spirit. What you look at the longest will become the focus of your life. The persistent are rewarded for their fervency in doing good and avoiding evil confrontations in this life. They know that no matter how rough their circumstances are, Jesus is always present as our protector, provider, and healer.

The woman with an issue of blood who pushed her way through the crowd to touch the hem of Jesus' garment, knew she would be healed from her 12 years of menstrual bleeding. Jesus' healing of her is one of His miracles in the gospels (see Matthew 9:20–22, Mark 5:25–34, and Luke 8:43–48). We, too, must know the healing powers of our faith in Jesus.

The seasons in our life will be more productive every time we use our faith. What you make happen for others, God will make happen for you. We must guard our minds with good things for ourselves and for others because **what we think of or dream can become a reality**. Our portal to prosperity increases with God's favor and blessings. He rewards us when we do good works for others, *"Give, and it will be given to you. Good measure, pressed down, shaken together, running over, will be put into your lap. For with the measure you use it will be measured back to you"* (Luke 6:38 ESV). ***"Truly I tell you, whatever you did for one of the least of these brothers and sisters of mine, you did for Me"*** **(Matthew 25:40 NIV).**

Chapter 8
CHARITY BRINGS GOD'S BLESSINGS TO THE GIVER

Jesus wants us to help those in need and does not want us to give begrudgingly but from our hearts. He wants us to be selfless and not selfish. He records all our good deeds and rewards us here in this life and in the hereafter. When we give to others, it must be with a cheerful heart and with the right motives.

Matthew 25:35 NIV

> *"For I was hungry, and you gave me something to eat. I was thirsty, and you gave me something to drink. I was a stranger, and you took me into your home."*

Matthew 25:40 KJV

> *"And the King shall answer and say unto them, verily I say unto you, inasmuch as ye have done it unto one of the least of these my brethren, ye have done it unto me."*

Isaiah 58:10 NLT

> *"Feed the hungry and help those in trouble. Then your light will shine out from the darkness, and the darkness around you will be as bright as noon."*

Romans 12:10 NASB

"Be devoted to one another in brotherly love; give preference to one another in honor."

Luke 11:41 KJV

"But give that which is within as charity, and then all things are clean for you."

Acts 20:35 NLT

*"And I have been a constant example of how you can help those in need by working hard. You should remember the words of the Lord Jesus: **it is more blessed to give than to receive.**"*

HELP THOSE IN NEED

Luke 12:33 ESV

"Sell your possessions, and give to the needy. Provide yourselves with moneybags that do not grow old, with a treasure in the heavens that does not fail, where no thief approaches and no moth destroys."

Philippians 2:3-4 ERV

"In whatever you do, don't let selfishness or pride be your guide. Be humble, and honor others more than yourselves. Don't be interested only in your own life, but care about the lives of others too."

Matthew 6:2 NLT

"When you give to someone in need, don't do as the hypocrites do—blowing trumpets in the synagogues and streets to call attention to their acts of charity! I tell you the truth, they have received all the reward they will ever get."

Luke 12:48 KJV

"But he that knew not, and did commit things worthy of stripes, shall be beaten with few stripes. For unto whomsoever much is given, of him shall be much required: and to whom men have committed much, of him they will ask the more."

2 Corinthians 9:8 GWT

"God will give you his constantly overflowing kindness. Then, when you always have everything you need, you can do more and more good things."

2 Corinthians 9:7 GWT

"Each of you should give whatever you have decided. You shouldn't be sorry that you gave or feel forced to give since God loves a cheerful giver."

Deuteronomy 15:10 NIV

"Give generously to them and do so without a grudging heart; then because of this the Lord your God will bless you in all your work and in everything you put your hand to."

Corinthians 13:3 GNT

"I may give away everything I have to help others, and I may even give my body as an offering to be burned. But I gain nothing by doing all this if I don't have love."

1 John 3:17 ESV

"If anyone has the world's goods and sees his brother in need, yet closes his heart against him, how does god's love abide in him?"

Proverbs 31:9 ESV

"Open thy mouth, judge righteously, and plead the cause of the poor and needy."

Chapter 9
OUR PASSIONS AND ACTIONS MUST ALIGN WITH GOD'S LAWS

The visionary adventurer nurtures a compelling passion for what he wants to produce during the course of his life. He knows his future is greater than his past and strives ahead to embrace life's amazing opportunities. His every goal complies with God's will and provides him with success, happiness, and fulfillment.

We should concentrate on today and tomorrow and forget about yesterday. We should always look forward to what lies ahead. Reaching forward should be every adventurer's goal. You cannot go forward looking back; you must keep your mind focus on your future, which can be so much greater than your past, especially as we grow and mature spiritually. Keep pushing and pressing to find what God has for you. Do not be bound by the past because it can dishonor your present and future. God has a storehouse of blessings that are overflowing for all of us. He is a loving God and wants the best for all of us. So, leave the past behind and forge ahead. Embrace God's blessings.

Your life is a picture of the decisions you made with your free will. Pray to our Father before making any and all decisions, because reaching your goals and materializing your ambitions depends on making the right decisions in life. What you chose to conquer, you will overcome. Your philosophy and faith create your lifestyle. When God created man, he gave him instructions and a free will. It is God's will that we adhere to his wise counsel and obey his Ten Commandments. He commands love and obedience. Our disobedience dishonors God. Always ask yourself, would God approve of me doing this? If it is in the will of God, then your path is paved in success. If it is not, don't do it because failure lurks behind making the wrong decision.

When you over-schedule your tasks, your attention will focus on those things you failed to accomplish, instead of being pleased with the tasks you have completed. How do you know what tasks should be undertaken? Ask yourself this question, "Is this going to be productive and necessary for my life?" It's essential we use the proper motives when we challenge ourselves to new under-takings. Even when we error, God is always with us. He never leaves or forsakes us, *Be strong and of good courage, fear not, nor be afraid of them: for the Lord thy God, he it is that doth go with thee; he will not fail thee, nor forsake thee*" (Deuteronomy 31:6 KJV).

Strife is proof that we are not in the will of God. None of us have a perfect life, but strife should be avoided when it interferes with our relationship with God. He must come before all our en-deavors. God wants, above all things, to give us prosperity and good health. *Beloved, I wish above all things that thou mayest prosper and be in health, even as thy soul prospereth*" (3 John 2:2 KJV).

If we choose not to honor God and his laws, it will flood out our blessings. Not everyone knows how to receive opportunity, correction, instruction, and favor. Don't put anything in front of you that doesn't inspire you because you will not give it your all. Failure will come because your intentions were not consistent with your desires and purposes. You have a responsibility to honor your integrity, not degrade it. It is your duty to inspire yourself. Without inspiration, you have no dreams, excitement, or energy.

You will always be remembered for either the problems you solve OR the problems you create.

Mastering the art of conversation is the most important communication skill we have in this world. God wants to communicate with us, and we should find the time to have a relationship with Him. When you do this, God will make things happen in your life, as He did for King David.

KING DAVID'S HEARTFELT WORDS TO GOD IN PSALM 145 (NLT)

"1 I will exalt you, my God and King, and praise your name forever and ever.

2 I will praise you every day; yes, I will praise you forever.

3 Great is the lord! He is most worthy of praise! No one can measure his greatness.

4 Let each generation tell its children of your mighty acts; let them proclaim your power.

5 I will meditate on your majestic, glorious splendor and your wonderful miracles.

6 Your awe-inspiring deeds will be on every tongue; I will proclaim your greatness.

7 Everyone will share the story of your wonderful goodness; they will sing with joy about your righteousness.

8 The Lord is merciful and compassionate, slow to get angry and filled with unfailing love.

9 The Lord is good to everyone. He showers compassion on all his creation.

10 All of your works will thank you, Lord, and your faithful followers will praise you.

11 They will speak of the glory of your kingdom; they will give examples of your power.

12 They will tell about your mighty deeds and about the majesty and glory of your reign.

13 For your kingdom is an everlasting kingdom. You rule throughout all generations.

14 The Lord always keeps his promises; he is gracious in all he does.

15 The Lord helps the fallen and lifts those bent beneath their loads.

16 The eyes of all look to you in hope; you give them their food as they need it.

17 When you open your hand, you satisfy the hunger and thirst of every living thing.

18 The Lord is righteous in everything he does; he is filled with kindness.

19 The Lord is close to all who call on him, yes, to all who call on him in truth.

20 He grants the desires of those who fear him; he hears their cries for help and rescues them.

21 The Lord protects all those who love him, but he destroys the wicked.

22 I will praise the Lord, and may everyone on earth bless his holy name forever and ever."

God blessed and favored David in his earthly life and made him king over Israel. He allowed the seed of the Messiah to come through his ancestral line. **God always inhabits the praises of those who love him.**

Chapter 10
GOD'S BLESSINGS ARE COUNTLESS

The seasons in your life will always be changing. Use your faith and watch it grow against all adversities. Recognition of the truth guarantees access to its treasures, with countless measures of wisdom as well. Failure is not an option, but an opinion. Singer, Dean Martin, made famous the song, *"Your Nobody Until Somebody Loves You*.**"** The moment you are conceived in your mother's womb, you are somebody, because God loves you!

The devil hates you and will try to destroy everything in your life. To do this, he must get into your mind. Only you can control what goes into your mind, not the devil. So, close your mind to him and his evil thoughts. Instead, open your mind to God's promises of love, peace, joy, and happiness. **You will only have what you chose to receive, whether it be good or bad.**

People never change what they believe, as long as their belief system produces something they want. Faith in God allows our belief system to function at high speed. No one, with the truth within them, can fail, because God showers His blessings and favors onto those who love Him. He despises those who disobey His Laws and reject His amazing grace of eternal salvation through His Son, Jesus.

Successful people keep worthy friendships and sift out those who are confrontational and non-productive to their life. Making positive decisions produces positive results. Everyone has limitations to deal with in this life, but confidence overcomes them all by allowing only good and productive thoughts to enter their minds. When God called Moses to go to the Pharaoh in Egypt to set his people free, Moses felt his stuttering speech would prevent him from doing this assignment. So, God instructed his brother Aaron to speak to the Pharaoh instead. As Aaron and Moses went forward together in this assignment, they witnessed all the miracles that God performed. Their faith, confidence, and relationship with God grew beyond measure. That was how Moses overcame his speech impediment and led God's people out of Egypt, out of bondage, and through the Red Sea. When we commune with God, He can use our personal limitations to bring us over the top. God will either bring a helpmate or an opportunity, to give us triumphs over our shortcomings and adversities just as he did with Moses.

The uncommon achiever is willing to go where he has never gone before by creating an environment that keeps him fully directed and stimulated regardless of adversities. Your reaction to grief and suffering reveals your humility and strength. Jesus warns us that in this life, we will have tribulations. He said, *"In the world ye shall have tribulation: but be of good cheer; I have overcome the world"* (John 16:33 KJV).Prior to his crucifixion, Jesus gave us the Blessed Assurance that He will never leave or forsake us, and, with his second imminent coming, He will rescue everyone who believes in Him and repents of their sins. *"Let your conversation be without covetousness; and be content with such things as ye have: for he hath said, **'I will never leave thee, nor forsake thee'**"* (Hebrews 13:5 KJV).

God blesses us so we can be a blessing to others. An act of disobedience increases the distance to any miracle you are pursuing.

Failure will last as long as you permit it. The essence of hope is in our faith. Confusion is proof that a deceiver is present. The smallest step in the wrong direction cheats our joy. Whatever you are willing to walk away from determines what God will bring to you. Anything good is hated by Satan. God's approval is necessary for anything you want to have work in your life. Never attempt anything without God's approval and blessing if you want true and lasting success. God rewards our faith in Him with life-saving power.

In this world, fear and warfare constantly lurk. However, with a strong mindset of God's precepts, you shall prevail over all spiritual attacks. Satan cannot linger where he is firmly resisted. Faith is confidence in the integrity of God. Your rewards in life are determined by the kinds of problems you are willing to solve for others and yourself. The Holy Spirit reveals inner peace with favor and opportunity to every believer in Jesus. You should not change your mind when it is in correct alignment with God and His Laws. **I know I am a child of God because, in my heart and mind, I only want to please Him.** The proof of God's presence far outweighs the falsehoods of His absence. Right words decide the longevity of every relationship. Reaching to help others is a very small price for what you receive. When warfare comes, your faith becomes a safe harbor. Unrest occurs when your spirit can't discern the truth. Your greatest enemy is always within you. Everything you need or want is from God. Understanding and dealing with life's challenges comes by staying in the Word and knowing you have the power of the indwelling of the Holy Spirit. When the right people enter your life, the right things begin to happen. **A fool is someone who makes the same mistakes repeatedly. You are not a fool when you learn by your mistakes and refuse to repeat them.**

God is always concerned with your personal prosperity and good health. *"Beloved, I pray that you may prosper in all things and be in health, just as your soul prospers"* **(3 John 2 NKJV).** It's your enemies who want to destroy your blessings and your financial harvest. **It is important that you chose the right people to associate and fellowship with**. It pleases the heart of God when we are evenly yoked with believers.

The biggest mountain will succumb to the smallest seed of faith. Jesus encourages us to have faith. *"If you have faith as a mustard seed, you can say to this mulberry tree, Be pulled up by the roots and be planted in the sea, and it would obey you"* **(Luke 17:6 NKJV). Jesus also encourages us to be positive in our thoughts and not to doubt.** *"If you have faith and do not doubt, you will not only do what has been done to the fig tree, but even if you say to this mountain, 'Be taken up and thrown into the sea,' it will happen"* **(Matthew 21:21 ESV).**

Satan wants you to trust in yourself, and be independent of God and his commandments as he did to Eve. He told Eve, *"For God knows that in the day you eat of it your eyes will be opened, and you will be like God, knowing good and evil"* (Genesis 3:5 NKJV). Satan's goal is to destroy your testimony of faith and turn you against God and his Ten Commandments. Every believer has the presence of God's Holy Spirit, which is THE most important relationship within you. He will instruct, guide, and teach you in all His ways. He is with you from conception and throughout all eternity.

In the *"garden of life,"* it is not the responsibility of the rose to remove the thorns. Obedience turns a common instruction into an uncommon miracle. Everything you need or want is already in your life, merely awaiting your recognition of it. Working for a living gives us a sense of giving back and being rewarded for our toil. Our labor gives us a sense of purpose and fulfillment.

The presence of God is the only place your weakness dies, and your gratitude flows continuously. What you respect will move toward you. Your faith decides your life experiences. The greater your assignment, the greater the demonic warfare will be. Greatness is simply fulfilling God's expectations of you — the greater your future, the longer your training. Fear is not normal; love is the power that dissolves fear. This is how you can recognize true love.

TEN BLESSINGS FOR WALKING IN GOD'S DIVINE FAVOR

1. SUPERNATURAL INCREASE AND PROMOTION

> *"But the Lord was with Joseph and showed him mercy, and He gave him favor in the sight of the keeper of the prison"* (Genesis 39:21 NKJV).

2. RESTORATION OF ALL THE ENEMY HAS STOLEN FROM YOU

> *"And I will give this people favor in the sight of the Egyptians; and it shall be, when you go, that you shall not go empty-handed"* (Exodus 3:21 NKJV).

3. HONOR IN THE MIDST OF YOUR ADVERSARIES

> *"And the Lord gave the people favor in the sight of the Egyptians. Moreover, the man Moses was very great in the land of Egypt, in the sight of Pharaoh's servants and in the sight of the people"* (Exodus 11:3 NKJV).

4. INCREASED ASSETS ESPECIALLY IN REAL ESTATE

> *"And of Naphtali, he said: 'O Naphtali, satisfied with favor, and full of the blessing of the Lord, possess the west and the south"* (Deuteronomy 33:23 NKJV).

5. GREATEST VICTORIES IN THE MIDST OF THE MOST

IMPOSSIBLE ODDS

"For it was of the Lord to harden their hearts, that they should come against Israel in battle, that He might utterly destroy them, and that they might receive no mercy, but that He might destroy them, as the Lord had commanded Moses" (Joshua 11:20 NKJV).

6. RECOGNITION EVEN WHEN YOU SEEM TO BE THE LEAST LIKELY TO RECEIVE IT

"Then Saul sent to Jesse, saying, "Please let David stand before me, for he has found favor in my sight" (1 Samuel 16:22 NKJV).

7. PROMINENCE AND PREFERENTIAL TREATMENT

"The king loved Esther more than all the other women, and she obtained grace and favor in his sight more than all the virgins; so he set the royal crown upon her head and made her queen instead of Vashti" (Ester 2:17 NKJV).

8. PETITIONS GRANTED EVEN BY UNGODLY AUTHORITIES

"If I have found favor in the sight of the king, and if it pleases the king to grant my petition and fulfill my request, then let the king and Haman come to the banquet which I will prepare for them, and tomorrow I will do as the king has said" (Esther 5:8 NKJV).

9. PUBLIC POLICIES, RULES, REGULATIONS, AND EVEN LAWS ARE CHANGED OR REVERSED TO YOUR ADVANTAGE

"If it pleases the king, and if I have found favor in his sight and the thing seems right to the king and I am pleasing in his eyes, let it be written to revoke the letters devised by Haman, the son of Hammedatha the Agagite, which he wrote to annihilate the Jews who are in all the king's provinces" (Ester 8:5 NKJV).

10. BATTLES WON IN WHICH YOU DO NOT EVEN HAVE TO FIGHT BECAUSE GOD WILL FIGHT THEM FOR YOU

"For they did not gain possession of the land by their own sword, nor did their own arm save them; But it was Your right hand, Your arm, and the light of Your countenance, because You favored them" (Psalm 44:3 NKJV).

GOD ALWAYS KEEPS HIS PROMISES

God keeps all his promises; He does not lie. He will never leave us or forsake us no matter what trials we go through in life. He will always be there for us to guide, direct, and support us through any and all trials, tribulations and adversities. **We must daily fortify ourselves with his Word because his promises are true and infallible.** He wants us to repent of our sins and have eternal life through his Son Jesus. We cannot conceive in our mind what God has in store for those who love Him *"No eye has seen, no ear has heard, and no mind has imagined what God has prepared for those who love him"* (1 Corinthians 2:9 NLT).

Hebrews 6:18 NLT

*"God has given both His promise and His oath. These two things are unchangeable because **it is impossible for God to lie.** Therefore, we who have fled to Him for refuge can have great confidence as we hold to the hope that lies before us."*

2 Corinthians 1:20 NKJV

"All the promises of God in Him are yes, and in Him Amen, to the glory of God through us."

Psalm 89:34 TLB

"No, I will not break My covenant; I will not take back one word of what I said."

Joshua 23:14 ESV

"Not one word has failed of all the good things that the Lord your God promised concerning you. All have come to pass for you; not one of them has failed."

1 John 2:25 NKJV

"This is the promise that He has promised us—eternal life."

Isaiah 49:25 NKJV

"I will contend with him who contends with you, and I will save your children."

Luke 18:27 NKJV

"The things which are impossible with men are possible with God.

Ezekiel 36:26 NKJV

"I will give you a new heart and put a new spirit within you; I will take the heart of stone out of your flesh and give you a heart of flesh.

1 John 1:9 NKJV

"If we confess our sins, He is faithful and just to forgive us our sins and to cleanse us from all unrighteousness."

Psalm 103:12 NKJV

"As far as the east is from the west, so far has He removed our transgressions from us."

Micah 7:19 NKJV

"He will again have compassion on us, and will subdue our iniquities. You will cast all our sins into the depths of the sea."

Galatians 5:22-23 NKJV

"The fruit of the Spirit is love, joy, peace, longsuffering, kindness, goodness, faithfulness, gentleness, self-control. Against such there is no law."

Luke 11:13 NKJV

"If you then, being evil, know how to give good gifts to your children, how much more will your heavenly Father give the Holy Spirit to those who ask Him!"

John 16:13 KJV

"When He, the Spirit of Truth, is come, He will guide you into all truth: for He shall not speak of Himself; but whatsoever He shall hear, that shall He speak: and He will shew you things to come."

Psalms 34:9-10NKJV

"Oh, fear the Lord, you His saints! There is no want to those who fear Him. The young lions lack and suffer hunger; but those who seek the Lord shall not lack any good thing."

Matthew 6:31-34 NKJV

"Therefore, do not worry, saying, 'What shall we eat?' or 'What shall we drink?' or 'What shall we wear?' for after all these things the Gentiles seek. For your heavenly Father knows that you need all these things. But seek first the kingdom of God and His right-

eousness, and all these things shall be added to you. Therefore, do not worry about tomorrow, for tomorrow will worry about its own things. Sufficient for the day is its own trouble."

Joshua 1:8 NKJV

"This book of the Law shall not depart from your mouth, but you shall meditate in it day and night, that you may observe to do according to all that is written in it. For then you will make your way prosperous, and then you will have good success."

Malachi 3:10-11 NKJV

"'Bring all the tithes into the storehouse, that there may be food in My house, and try Me now in this,' says the Lord of Hosts, 'if I will not open for you the windows of heaven and pour out for you such blessing that there will not be room enough to receive it. and I will rebuke the devourer for your sakes, so that he will not destroy the fruit of your ground, nor shall the vine fail to bear fruit for you in the field,' says the Lord of Hosts.'"

Philippians 4:19 NKJV

"My God shall supply all your need according to His riches in glory by Christ Jesus."

Romans 8:32 NKJV

"He who did not spare His own Son, but delivered Him up for us all, how shall He not with Him also freely give us all things?"

Psalm 84:11 TLB

"Jehovah God is our light and our protector. He gives us grace and glory. No good thing will He withhold from those who walk along His paths."

Jeremiah 30:17 NKJV

"'I will restore health to you and heal you of your wounds,' says the Lord."

Exodus 15:26 NKJV

"If you diligently heed the voice of the Lord, your God and do what is right in His sight, give ear to His commandments and keep all His statutes, I will put none of the diseases on you which I have brought on the Egyptians. For I am the Lord, who heals you."

Psalms 103:2-3 NKJV

"Bless the Lord, O my soul, and forget not all His benefits: Who forgives all your iniquities, Who heals all your diseases."

James 1:5 NKJV

"If any of you lacks wisdom, let him ask of God, who gives to all liberally and without reproach, and it will be given to him."

Psalms 32:8 KJV

"I will instruct thee and teach thee in the way which thou shalt go: I will guide thee with mine eye."

Proverbs 3:5-7 NKJV

"Trust in the Lord with all your heart, and lean not on your own understanding; in all your ways acknowledge Him, and He shall direct your paths. Do not be wise in your own eyes; fear the Lord and depart from evil."

Isaiah 30:21 KJV

"Thine ears shall hear a word behind thee, saying, this is the way, walk ye in it, when ye turn to the right hand, and when ye turn to the left."

Isaiah 49:25 NKJV

"I will contend with him who contends with you, and I will save your children."

Psalms 127:3-5 NKJV

"Behold, children are a heritage from the Lord, the fruit of the womb is a reward. Like arrows in the hand of a warrior, so are the children of one's youth. Happy is the man who has his quiver full of them; they shall not be ashamed, but shall speak with their enemies in the gate."

Isaiah 26:3 NKJV

"You will keep him in perfect peace, whose mind is stayed on you, because he trusts in you."

Psalm 119:165 NKJV

"Great peace have those who love Your law, and nothing causes them to stumble."

1 Corinthians 10:13 NKJV

"No temptation has overtaken you except such as is common to man; but God is faithful, who will not allow you to be tempted beyond what you are able, but with the temptation will also make the way of escape, that you may be able to bear it."

James 4:7-10 NKJV

"Therefore, submit to God. Resist the devil and he will flee from you. Draw near to God and He will draw near to you. Cleanse your hands, you sinners; and purify your hearts, you double-minded. Lament and mourn and weep! Let your laughter be turned to mourning and your joy to gloom. Humble yourselves in the sight of the Lord, and He will lift you up."

Hebrews 2:18 NKJV

"For in that He Himself has suffered, being tempted, He is able to aid those who are tempted."

Psalm 91:4-6 NKJV

"He shall cover you with His feathers, and under His wings, you shall take refuge; His truth shall be your shield and buckler. You shall not be afraid of the terror by night, nor of the arrow that flies by day, nor of the pestilence that walks in darkness, nor of the destruction that lays waste at noonday."

Psalm 138:7 NKJV

"Though I walk in the midst of trouble, You will revive me; You will stretch out Your hand against the wrath of my enemies, and Your right hand will save me."

Psalm 34:4 NKJV

"I sought the Lord, and He heard me, and delivered me from all my fears."

John 14:27 NKJV

"Peace I leave with you, My peace I give to you; not as the world gives do I give to you. Let not your heart be troubled, neither let it be afraid."

John 5:28-29 NKJV

"Do not marvel at this; for the hour is coming in which all who are in the graves will hear His voice and come forth—those who have done good, to the resurrection of life, and those who have done evil, to the resurrection of condemnation."

John 14:2-3 NKJV

In My Father's house are many mansions; if it were not so, I would have told you. I go to prepare a place for you. And if I go and prepare a place for you, I will come again and receive you to Myself; that where I am, there you may be also."

1 Thessalonians 4:15-18 NKJV

"For this, we say to you by the Word of the Lord, that we who are alive and remain until the coming of the Lord will by no means precede those who are asleep. For the Lord, himself will descend from heaven with a shout, with the voice of an archangel, and with the trumpet of God. And the dead in Christ will rise first. Then we who are alive and remain shall be caught up together with them in the clouds to meet the Lord in the air. And thus, we shall always be with the Lord. Therefore comfort one another with these words."

Revelation 21:4 NKJV

"God will wipe away every tear from their eyes; there shall be no more death, nor sorrow, nor crying. There shall be no more pain, for the former things have passed away."

Chapter 11
THE LAW OF RECOGNITION

The Law of Recognition is when one hears the voice of the Holy Spirit, who gives us God's assignment. His voice can be heard anytime, anywhere, and in any geographical region. Listen to God's counsel and never take advice from a fool, who will not only mislead you but himself as well. Never invest your time or take counsel with a fool. When you stop listening, He will stop talking. When you ask God for a future event, Satan will put a fool in your path. Discard all negative relationships. Search for a spiritual intercessor as David did with the prophet Nathan, and King Solomon did with prophet Saul. The devil will only produce fools and deceivers in your life. God produces his Holy Spirit and those who hear His prophetic counsel.

Do not be boastful; let others compliment you instead. One who is insistent on his own views will find few who will agree with him or support him in his endeavors. Every leader has a Judas. Jesus did, and you will too. Know your weak points and your strengths. Praying and believing in God is always wise. Depending and trusting in others is unwise. When you have an enemy in your circle, be cautious because their goal is to mess up you and your life.

When God gives you an assignment, it is surrounded by His wisdom and power. He will give you ample provisions to accomplish His divinely inspired tasks. Trust in your salvation because God guarantees it. **When the past calls to remind you of your faults and failures, push the ignore button because they have nothing new to say, and no good ever comes from reflecting on your non-achievements**. Instead, you must go forward and learn from past mistakes and never look back.

Having endurance will bring you to victory. Expect an uncommon anointing, and you will receive miracles. Our self-portrait of God's blessings determines our self-conduct and rewards. You will never possess what you are unwilling to acknowledge or pursue. Do not be afraid of going slowly and cautiously forward, only of standing still. Dismantle your fears and do not allow them to overpower you. *"Fear not, for I am with you; Be not dismayed, for I am your God. I will strengthen you, Yes, I will help you, I will uphold you with My righteous right hand"* **(Isaiah 41:10 NKJV)**.The greatest weapon against fear, which causes one stress, is our ability to renew our minds and choose a positive thought over a negative one. *"Do not be conformed to this world, but be transformed by the renewing of your mind, that you may prove what is that good and acceptable and perfect will of God"* (Romans 12:2 NKJV).

Before a bird can fly, he has to break out of its shell. From the day we are born until we take our last breath, we go through the ever-changing portals of life. There are growing processes and adjustments we all must make as we journey through life. Every day we are growing and expanding our horizons. Our will leads us to our final destiny. We need God to guide us so we can grow and prosper in all of our endeavors. King David prayed, *"Show me your ways, Lord, teach me your paths. Guide me in your truth and teach me, for you are God my Savior, and my hope is in you all day long"* **(Psalm 25:4-5 NIV)**.

Satan is ever-present in our growth process, wanting to turn us away from God, His laws, and His guidance. When we meet up with obstacles, we must follow God and not Satan. Avoid fellowship with those who do not honor God. They rarely become trustworthy because they follow the gods of this world. We all must choose who we will serve in this life, and it's either God or Satan *"Choose for yourselves this day whom you will serve, whether the gods which your fathers served that were on the other side of the River, or the gods of the Amorites, in whose land you dwell. **But as for me and my house, we will serve the Lord"*** (Joshua 24:15 NKJV).

Chapter 12
BIBLICAL SCRIPTURES ON HEALING

Even though everyone experiences physical and emotional pain in their life, God wants to heal our body and broken spirit. He sent His son, Jesus, to spread the Good News of the Gospel and to heal the sick, the dying, and broken-hearted. The most important thing to realize is that everyone can receive healing to their body, mind, and spirit.

Mark 9:23 KJV

"Jesus said unto him, 'If thou canst believe, all things are possible to him that believeth.'"

Luke 8:50 KJV

"But when Jesus heard it, He answered him, saying, 'Fear not: believe only, and she shall be made whole.'"

Psalm 147:3 KJV

"He healeth the broken in heart, and bindeth up their wounds."

Mark 10:52 KJV

"And Jesus said unto him, 'Go thy way; thy faith hath made thee whole.' And immediately he received his sight, and followed Jesus in the way."

James 5:14-15 KJV

"Is any sick among you? Let him call for the elders of the church; and let them pray over him, anointing him with oil in the name of the Lord: and the prayer of faith shall save the sick, and the Lord shall raise him up; and if he have committed sins, they shall be forgiven him."

James 5:16 KJV

"Confess your faults one to another, and pray one for another, that ye may be healed. The effectual fervent prayer of a righteous man availeth much."

Matthew 10:8 KJV

"Heal the sick, cleanse the lepers, raise the dead, cast out devils: freely ye have received, freely give."

2 Chronicles 7:14 KJV

"A merry heart doeth good like a medicine: but a broken spirit drieth the bones."

Malachi 4:2 KJV

"But unto you that fear My name shall the Sun of righteousness arise with healing in His wings; and ye shall go forth, and grow up as calves of the stall."

Isaiah 53:5 KJV

"But he was wounded for our transgressions, he was bruised for our iniquities: the chastisement of our peace was upon him; and with his stripes we are healed."

1 Peter 2:24 KJV

"Who His own self bare our sins in His own body on the tree, that we, being dead to sins, should live unto righteousness: by whose stripes ye were healed."

2 Kings 20:5 KJV

"Turn again, and tell Hezekiah the captain of My people, thus saith the Lord, the God of David thy Father, I have heard thy prayer, I have seen thy tears: behold, I will heal thee: on the third day thou shalt go up unto the house of the Lord."

Luke 10:9 KJV

"And heal the sick that are therein, and say unto them, 'The Kingdom of God is come nigh unto you.'"

Luke 13:10-17 KJV

"And He was teaching in one of the synagogues on the sabbath. And, behold, there was a woman which had a spirit of infirmity eighteen years, and was bowed together, and could in no wise lift up herself. And when Jesus saw her, He called her to Him, and said unto her, 'Woman, thou art loosed from thine infirmity.' And He laid His hands on her: and immediately she was made straight, and glorified God. And the ruler of the synagogue answered with indignation, because that Jesus had healed on the sabbath day, and said unto the people, 'There are six days in which men ought to work: in them therefore come and be healed, and not on the sab-

bath day.' The Lord then answered him, and said, 'Thou hypocrite, doth not each one of you on the sabbath loose his ox or his ass from the stall, and lead him away to watering? And ought not this woman, being a daughter of Abraham, whom Satan hath bound, lo, these eighteen years, be loosed from this bond on the sabbath day?' And when He had said these things, all His adversaries were ashamed: and all the people rejoiced for all the glorious things that were done by Him."

Matthew 9:12 KJV

"If thou wilt diligently hearken to the voice of the Lord thy God, and wilt do that which is right in His sight, and wilt give ear to His commandments, and keep all His statutes, I will put none of these diseases upon thee, which I have brought upon the Egyptians: for I am the Lord that healeth thee."

Luke 4:18 KJV

"The Spirit of the Lord is upon Me, because He hath anointed Me to preach the gospel to the poor; He hath sent Me to heal the brokenhearted, to preach deliverance to the captives, and recovery of sight to the blind, to set at liberty them that are bruised."

Chapter 13
GOD'S SALVATION FOR MANKIND IS ONLY THROUGH JESUS

Dear Jesus,

Thank you for the brand-new life you gave me when you died on the cross on Calvary. You died for all my sins. I accept Your sacrifice and repent of all my sins. I know I am now a new creation, and my sins are forever washed away. [*"Therefore, if anyone is in Christ, he is a new creation; old things have passed away; behold, all things have become new"* (2 Corinthians 5:17 NKJV).] Everyone and everything were created by You. We are greatly blessed through Your saving grace. In You, we have the eternal presence of the Holy Spirit, who gives us the power and authority to cast out demons and bind them and every form of evil. We know that obedience is the seed for our blessings and that God responds to our tears and our pain, but always reacts to our faith. You gave us the promise that whatsoever we ask the Father in Your name. He will do it. [*"If you ask anything in My name, I will do it"* (John 14:14 NKJV).] Satan plants the seed of doubt to weaken our faith. But Your life, death, and resurrection gives us the Blessed Assurance of eternal life and washes away all doubt and uncertainties. Our shield of faith can and does extinguish all the flaming darts of Satan. A man without faith is a man without hope. A man without hope is a man with no motivation to fulfill his destiny for God or for himself. Jesus, You gave us Your divine peace. Soon, you will lead us to our eternal home in heaven, where we will live forever with You, our Heavenly Father, the Holy Spirit, and all our saved loved ones!

Amen

Our greatest blessing comes from belonging to the Son of God, Jesus Christ, our Lord and Savior, who gave His life to save everyone from their sins. When we believe in Him and repent of our sins, He gives us eternal salvation. Jesus wants us as his bride, without spot or wrinkle, to be in a marriage relationship with Him, which He has divinely instituted. This is the beginning of the greatest peace and contentment we have here on earth, where we are wrapped in love and secured with our faith. A revival is coming to this world to clear the way for the bride of Christ, so the Royal Groom can receive His bride (believers) who are longing for His soon return.

According to Bible prophecy, the current world events signal His imminent second coming. **We are the generation that will witness the countdown to the end of these final days. No man knows the hour or the day, but scripture does give us the season. We are in that season, as all Bible prophesies predict, because the end of days are now here!**

A real river of wisdom will find intelligence swimming there. Never reveal your strategy against your enemy to those uncommitted to you and your case. *"A fool uttereth all his mind: but a wise man keepeth it in till afterwards"* **(Proverbs 29:11 KJV).** A person is operating under legalistic law will always produce anger. The successful lifelong learner isn't immune to challenges, setbacks, nor even sufferings. In fact, it is something they've learned to deal with on a consistent basis. But any and all resistance they meet only strengthens their resolve to keep pressing forward. This makes them stronger and more resilient as they continue to advance forcefully in the face of adversity with staying power that is remarkable. They refuse to quit because they are divinely fueled. This is a trait one must master even when the enemy puts you down. If you seem to lose some things, know if you persevere, **you will get it all back with interest!**

When evil forces try to keep you from being your best, and fulfilling your destiny and those around you offer no cooperation, keep moving forward, because God is with you and wants the best for you. Do not give up your dreams or turn them loose. Never consult your past about your future. If you have not experienced radical change, write down what you want and activate your plans by speaking God's words of affirmation and include whatever your dreams and goals are. This could be a new home furnished with your favorite items, a brand-new wardrobe, a new job, earning more money for sowing, or a ministry in helping others. It could be anything your heart desires. God promises if we, *"Delight yourself also in the Lord, And He shall give you the desires of your heart"* **(Psalm 37:4 NKJV).**

Have a self-portrait of whatever you want with a picture showing a bright tomorrow so that a bright yesterday is too ashamed to show up. We should celebrate each and every day because life is truly a gift. There is no guarantee of tomorrow, so let everyday count. Keep multiplying your faith in God by staying in the Word, *"So then faith comes by hearing, and hearing by the Word of God"* **(Romans 10:17 NKJV).**

Always be who you were meant to be and set your mind on everything good and acceptable to God, then every day will be a day of peace, joy, and happiness filled with blessings that will override all the negative effects of our life's daily trials. *"And do not be conformed to this world, but be transformed by the renewing of your mind, that you may prove what is that good and acceptable and perfect will of God"* (Romans 12:2 NKJV).

Dear God, Our Heavenly Father,
We thank You for all Your blessings and favor. Help us to be kind and helpful in comforting others. Strengthen our love as we reach out to those in need. Give us the knowledge of what to do to stand firm and proud of our faith in You and what You have done for humanity. Always keep us stable, mature, and obedient to Your commandments, and honor Your being with praise and worship, while stretching beyond our own imagination with faith. We ask this in the name of Jesus."
Amen

God calls us to be whole and connected to Him and to follow the Holy Spirit's guiding light through life. He will never lead us astray or plot our ruin, *"I will never leave you nor forsake you"* **(Hebrews 13:5 NKJV).** None of us seeks loneliness. We were made to partner with God and each other. Helen Keller, the famous deaf and blind American author, political activist, and lecturer said these profound words, **"No one wants to go through this life alone. Walking with a friend in the dark is better than walking alone in the light."**

He who has much is rich, but he who gives much is richer. Medicine can cure the man who is fated to die. Death is the doorway to an eternity in either heaven or hell. The life-long learner has developed a deep love for wisdom. Over the course of their life, they become steadfast by honoring the timeless truths that shape noble core values. Their choices are governed by what is deeply engraved in their souls. They are not fooled nor enslaved by falsehoods, and they know that kindness and truth are their constant companions and that God's favor is consistently a factor in every aspect of their life. They don't give up. They don't go backward. They don't give in. They keep moving forward even when major obstacles are in their path. Their deepest desires are always to win and not to lose. Michael Jordan, a former professional basketball player, said, **"Talent wins games, but teamwork and intelligence win championships."**

Eliminate fleeting desires that offer no lasting satisfaction or fulfillment. Harness the passion to accomplish your objectives by using deliberate and determined actions. Focus on paying attention without distractions. This will magnify success for: 1. You, 2. People you need, 3. People who motivate you, 4. People who comfort you, 5. People who mentor you, 6. People who trust you, 7. People who criticize you, 8. People who enjoy you, 9. People who exploit you, and 10. People who admire you.

Chapter 14
THREE SPIRITUAL LETTERS TO DAUGHTERS ON RELATIONSHIPS

Dear Daughter,

The greatest contentment is knowing that the right person meant for your life was given to you by God. His initial interest is decided by your words, which keeps him listening. This will lead to a relationship. He will unleash his interest and communicate with you. When he is pleased, going forward will be inevitable. Any negative connotations will short circuit his ability to forge ahead in the relationship. Know that a good man never judges a woman by her beauty, only her ability to motivate him, which will make him stay longer in her presence. Life is like scholastic classes where you learn lessons on how to make positive things happen in your life.

You will never really know someone until you listen to their innermost thoughts and desires. When you are in a close relationship with someone, emotions, feelings, passion, and pleasure can often be contained in the same package. An irreplaceable husband knows his wife's inner and most painful thoughts, memories, and understands her decisions. She then becomes indispensable because she knows her husband's goals and supports him 100%.

Most men don't really want a lot, but what they do want, they will not live without! No man stays silent if you are discussing what he loves. Build a nest to energize him, and he will never stray. No man needs the same thing, desires the same thing, or pursues the same thing. Focus on his uniqueness and difference. You can do this because hope, to make this friendship work, resides within you.

The devil will try to strip away your faith and aspirations for a lasting relationship. The Bible promises, if we resist the devil, he will flee from us. *"Therefore submit to God. Resist the devil and he will flee from you"* (James 4:7 NKJV). We can accomplish this by allowing God's Word to rule our lives and our relationships with others. The Holy Spirit, who dwells in every believer, gives us discernment to know when Satan's evil head surfaces and the ability to avoid his temptations. Read the Bible and seek wisdom. This equips us to battle successfully all of Satan's wiles and having victory over life's countless challenges. Protect your mind from all negative thoughts, cast them away before their roots are planted. When we avoid temptation, we resist sin. Keep a humble spirit, and do not allow it to grow into conceit. Never allow your soul to be carried away. Stay focused on God and constantly commune with Him and, ***"pray without ceasing"*** (1 Thessalonians 5:17 NKJV).

Tell yourself that from now on, your decisions must include listening to the prompting of God's Holy Spirit, who resides within you 24/7. He places in you God's plan for living your life to the fullest and feeds and sustains you with positive affirmations that will guide you through life. He gives you the knowledge that you are God's child and promises protection from every evil demonic attachment, and any and all weapons formed against you: *"No weapon that is formed against thee shall prosper; and every tongue that shall rise against thee in judgment thou shalt condemn. This is the heritage of the servants of the Lord, and their righteousness is of me, saith the Lord"* (Isaiah 54:17 KJV).

Our words possess power. Negative words can become a reality and be the trap that ensnares us. There is power in the word. We must always think and speak affirmations of what is good and keep only positive thoughts in our minds. We should stay motivated with our faith in God and delete all negative thinking. There's power in our tongue to speak life or death! *"Death and life are in the power of the tongue"* (Proverbs 18:21 NKJV). To stay motivated, we must use our faith and the God-given power of our words to speak only good things to occur in our lives and in the lives of others!

Dear Daughter,

Your desire to please the man in your life reveals your character. To keep the relationship in a positive mode requires thoughtfulness. The right one can emerge as you strive towards your goals. Anything you fail to recognize or respect will eventually exit your life. The most valuable person in your life is the one who respects your faith. The proof of love is the investment of your time with that person, and wisdom is the ability to recognize it. Your best days are ahead, and your worst days are behind you. Wisdom is the ability to recognize who or what actually dominates your life. Whatever you are willing to settle for determines the quality of your future. Love without fear is filled with countless blessings. Always be equally yoked with the one you give your heart to and who honors your same beliefs and values.

If a woman knows how to talk to a man, that man will listen to her forever. Quality questions need forethought. When a man discerns a true listener, he never leaves. I have never met a man that was turned off by humility. Never confuse your mind because your mind is your servant. Don't expect a *"Mercedes marriage"* from a *"Honda courtship."* If you want a man, learn his thoughts, his needs, and his desires. Sex was created by God between a husband and a wife for procreating his family, and enjoyment as well. Sex should never be misused or abused, nor engaged in outside of marriage. The most valuable person in your life is the one who honors and respects your faith and your calling.

Wisdom is for those eager to learn. We all desire the process of growth, even when we struggle, and our heart is breaking. Speak to your future with positive thoughts. Leave behind the former things, and make room for the new. *"Do not remember the former things, Nor consider the things of old. Behold, I will do a new thing, Now it shall spring forth; Shall you not know it? I will even make a road in the wilderness And rivers in the desert"* **(Isaiah 43:18-19 NKJV).**

Confidence comes to those who you can live outside their comfort zone. Every problem is solvable if we focus on the solutions. Asking enough questions helps educate our minds. **Believing in God and his Word is the key to life.** The goal of an enemy is to change your self-direction and hinder your focus of going forward. Only in the Word of God can one find lasting truth, which continually nourishes our spirit. **Revenge fixates your energy and causes you to move backward.** This is never a wise thing to do. Give it to God and let him handle it and get on with your life. He warns: *"Dearly beloved, avenge not yourselves, but rather give place unto wrath: for it is written, Vengeance is Mine; I will repay, saith the Lord"* (Romans 12:19 KJV).

True change occurs when we embrace God's wisdom. The noble adventurer will march into hell for a heavenly cause and never embrace a process that leads to the death of one's soul. Without applying God's wisdom, one can cause their deepest fears to surface. With our faith held firmly in God, we can face our toughest challenges with success and conquer the strongest enemies. To rise above all adversities, one must have the power of insight and perseverance.

Dear Daughter,

A man will always listen to a woman if she talks about what's on his mind. Love is the thirst within us to mate with the one person who will be obsessed with being one with your soul and desires to please that one person for the rest of their life. One of the most important things in this world is communication. Master it. A man does not marry a woman for the way she looks, but for how he feels in her presence. **Loneliness is not the absence of affection but the absence of direction. Going forward with life eliminates attention to being alone.** Love is the relentless passion for pleasing another. Success is a collection of our achievements of what we have been called to pursue and accomplish.

It takes time for even a small cut to heal. Nevertheless, all healing is a process. Don't be distracted by the winds and waves. You must keep your focus on wisdom, knowing what to tolerate and what to terminate. Prohibit the accuser of the brethren, the devil, to influence your thoughts with anything or anyone who does not come into agreement with God. We must declare, "I reverse the effect of any evil stigmas, and declare God's divine favor, grace, honor, and blessings over me and everyone. I pray God will destroy any and all negative feelings, emotions, and thoughts in my life as well as everyone else's life! In the name of Jesus. Amen."

Chapter 15
GOD SENDS A HELPMATE INTO OUR LIFE

To help fulfill our purpose in this life, God will send us a helpmate. The Bible story of Ruth not wanting to leave her mother-in-law, Naomi, after both their husbands died, helped her to fulfill her own destiny. Her servant's heart made her stand in a place of breakthrough where she found her future helpmate. Ruth gave faithful and loving service to her mother-in-law, which was met with her restored happiness of a peaceful and prosperous new life. Through Naomi, she met her first husband's kinsman, Boaz. They married, and the seed of the Lord Jesus Christ passed through their union. Amminadab was the father of Nahshon, Nahshon was the father of Salmon, Salmon was the father of Boaz, Boaz was the father of Obed, Obed was the father of Jesse, Jesse was the father of David, (see Ruth 4:21-22) and Jesus Christ our Lord and Savior was born of the seed of David according to the flesh. *"Concerning his Son Jesus Christ our Lord, which was made of the seed of David according to the flesh"* (Romans 1:3 KJV).

Crying over life takes up time, energy, and does not leave room for fulfilling our purpose. Know that, in the Lord, all trials and tribulations lead to triumphs and victories. This strengthens us for a higher purpose. Associating with the wrong people, whether it be for business, personal, or otherwise, will not fulfill your purpose. In fact, it could detour you from fulfilling your goals and obtaining your rightful destiny. We are commanded not to be unevenly yoked with non-believers, ***"Do not be unequally yoked together with unbelievers. For what fellowship has righteousness with lawlessness? And what communion has light with darkness?"* (2 Corinthians 6:14 NKJV)**

Read the Bible and, *"pray without ceasing"* (1 Thessalonians 5:17 NKJV).God will reveal His plan for your life and give you what you need to fulfill your destiny. Be productive, think ahead. Move with the seasons and time. Everyone has a calling; some may go into sports, politics, entertainment, or a professional endeavor. When you find it, it fits well in your life. No one can stop you when you're fulfilling your calling from God. Those who oppose you will flee to others who they can control and manipulate because misery loves company. Believe in yourself. Do not consider what others may or may not be doing. It's none of your concern or business! You have all you can do to fulfill your own purpose and destiny. Take your eyes off people and concentrate on what God has called you to do to fulfill his purpose for your life, no matter how long or short it may be. (see John 15:1-6)

Chapter 16
MAKE MINDFUL CHOICES

When you ask God for a future, Satan will give you an enemy to overcome before reaching your destiny. In the Kingdom Principle, those who overcome adversity know that failure is not a possibility. If you take the time to study the challenges you are going through, you will learn things that you can't learn from books. **Your life will always move in the direction of your strongest thoughts. What you keep thinking in your mind, you will create it in your life.**

MAKE WISE DECISIONS:

Deuteronomy 30:19 (NLT)

"Today I have given you the choice between life and death, between blessings and curses. Now I call on heaven and earth to witness the choice you make. Oh, that you would choose life, so that you and your descendants might live!"

Romans 12:2 (NLT)

"Don't copy the behavior and customs of this world, but let God transform you into a new person by changing the way you think. Then you will learn to know God's will for you, which is good and pleasing and perfect."

2 Timothy 1:7 (NLT)

"God has not given us a spirit of fear and timidity, but of power, love, and self-discipline."

2 Corinthians 10:5 (ESV)

"We destroy arguments and every lofty opinion raised against the knowledge of God, and take every thought captive to obey Christ."

Philippians 4:8 (ESV)

"Whatever is true, whatever is honorable, whatever is just, whatever is pure, whatever is lovely, whatever is commendable, if there is any excellence, if there is anything worthy of praise, think about these things."

Proverbs 23:7 (NASB)

"For as he thinks within himself, so he is."

The greatest waste of time in ones' life is never to achieve your potential. If you think you can't, you won't. If you think you can, you will. **You can achieve whatever you put in your heart and mind if you maintain a positive mindset.**

Chapter 17
GOD'S PLAN FOR YOUR LIFE

God has a plan for everyone's life. He can do more with remains than man can do with ~~the~~ excess. If we keep our faith in God, the worst day in our future will be greater than the best day of our past. *"'For I know the plans I have for you,' declares the Lord, 'plans to prosper you and not to harm you, plans to give you hope and a future'"* (Jeremiah 29:11 NIV).

Love, romance, respect, and honor are seeds that produce a happy marriage. This also creates a healthy and happy family life with unending bliss and joy. Obedience to God's Laws creates a sound foundation with countless blessings as we journey through life. A good example of this is the Biblical account of Ruth's marriage to Boaz, which was divine intervention. Ruth had to be present in Boaz's field, where he saw and admired her virtues and her devotion to her mother in law, Naomi. God blessed their marriage with the seed of our Messiah that came through their union. Trust in God for the one to whom you are assigned to be with. He will bring the one you are qualified to partner with. Together, you will honor and respect each other as you both grow spiritually and live according to God's Laws and your marriage vows.

Walking towards your destiny will determine your wisdom. Wisdom determines your success. Employers who hire those with talent and wisdom will increase their own success in business. Wealth may purchase a house, but wisdom makes it a home. We must view change as an adventure with something significant to gain. Begin exploring the many benefits of embracing those changes, because it is a sign pointing and guiding you forward to your goals and destiny. When your scenery and everything you are familiar with is changing, you are experiencing growth. If your scenery stays the same, you are stalled and become stagnate. Change is good and sometimes painful, but it always advances and propels us to a new season. Don't allow fear to cause you not to make changes in your life.

You should always team with the best people possible to win control over any and all adversities. The greater the inner resistance you experience, the more profound the change is, which needs to take place. See change as an adventure with something significant to gain. Begin to explore the many benefits of embracing change. Mastering the ability to change misbeliefs requires an effective method of casting them out of your mind and preventing yourself from ever having them reoccur. Listening to misbeliefs will only lead to giving them mind power. Mastering them requires facing the hold they have on you. Talk back to them powerfully. Tell yourself what is God's truth and replace those misbeliefs with the fact you are a conqueror and can do all things through Christ, who strengthens you. (see Philippians 4:13). Jesus is much more powerful than the devil. He washes away all the devil's temptations of evil thoughts, desires, and misbeliefs.

It is important to use our time wisely because it takes time to manage our life productively. Change is essential when you enter a new phase or stage of your life's journey. Every promotion involves having to master new skills quickly successfully and resourcefully. Security lurks in the shadows of these seasons. The intensity of learning is tied to each new venture. Let your heart embrace the notion that you will succeed in all your ventures. Do not harbor doubt. **Reaffirm, "I will triumph in this course, and I will develop new skills to succeed in this new endeavor."** Work hard and be devoted, and you will reap all the benefits of your success. There is no magic science in obtaining prosperity. It is what God wants for all of us to be successful and in good health. *"Beloved, I pray that you may prosper in all things and be in health, just as your soul prospers"* (3 John 2 NKJV). We should always strive to fulfill our destiny and know that God will bless all our efforts. **We must abide in Him and keep His Commandments**

THE LORD DETERMINES OUR STAGES IN LIFE AND DIRECTS OUR STEPS

"'For I know the plans I have for you,' declares the Lord, 'plans to prosper you and not to harm you, plans to give you hope and a future'" (Jeremiah 29:11 NIV).

"A man's heart deviseth his way: but the Lord directeth his steps" (Proverbs 16:9 KJV).

GOD REWARDS THOSE WHO KEEP HIS TEN COMMANDMENTS

"He who has My commandments and keeps them, it is he who loves Me. And he who loves Me will be loved by My Father, and I will love him and manifest Myself to him" (John 14:21 NKJV).

GOD WILL DWELL WITH THOSE WHO KEEP HIS WORDS

"If anyone loves Me, he will keep My word; and My Father will love him, and We will come to him and make Our abode with him" (John 14:23 NASB).

WE WILL ABIDE IN GOD'S LOVE, AND OUR JOY WILL BE FULL

"If you keep My commandments, you will abide in My love, just as I have kept My Father's commandments and abide in His love. These things I have spoken to you, that My joy may remain in you, and that your joy may be full" (John 15:10-11 NKJV).

WE WILL KNOW GOD IF WE KEEP HIS COMMANDMENTS

"Now by this we know that we know Him, if we keep His commandments. He who says, 'I know Him,' and does not keep His commandments, is a liar, and the truth is not in him. But whoever keeps His word, truly the love of God is perfected in him. By this we know that we are in Him" (1 John 2:3-5).

"If you love Me, keep My commandments" (John 14:15 NKJV).

WE SHOW GOD LOVE WHEN WE KEEP HIS COMMANDMENTS

"By this we know that we love the children of God, when we love God and keep His commandments" (1 John 5:2).

WE ARE FRIENDS OF CHRIST WHEN WE OBEY HIS COMMAND

"You are My friends if you do whatever I command you" (John 15:14).

OUR PRAYERS ARE ANSWERED WHEN WE OBEY GOD'S COMMANDMENTS

"And whatever we ask we receive from Him, because we keep His commandments and do those things that are pleasing in His sight" (1 John 3:22).

WE ARE TRUE DISCIPLES OF JESUS WHEN WE LOVE GOD AND EACH OTHER

"A new commandment I give to you, that you love one another; as I have loved you, that you also love one another. By this all will know that you are My disciples, if you have love for one another" (John 13:34-35).

Chapter 18
RESPECT YOUR GOD-GIVEN ASSIGNMENT

Those who disrespect your divine assignments are disqualified for your friendship. You don't have to change for them, because God's will is that you conform to him and not man. It's important to keep friendships with those who are in alignment with your calling. Do not be unevenly yoked with non-believers; they can mar your path with major stumbling blocks" (2 Corinthians 6:14 NKJV).

When people say something positive to build you up, it empowers your confidence. If they say something that is not constructive and is cruel and hurtful, know that this is from a dark place. You should disown those relationships; they are only meant to tear you down. When we walk in God's favor and allow our faith to grow, we can do all the things we are appointed to do. (see Philippians 4:13-17) Learn to develop and strengthen your skills and talents. Do not easily get distracted by the chatter of others or let life give you anything but joy and peace. Savor every moment because your life is a blessing from God. Demand this for yourself, and you will achieve your heart's desires. Be ready and prepared to do whatever God anoints you to do.

We must pray for what we need to fulfill our destiny. King Solomon prayed for wisdom to rule God's people, and God gave him great wisdom. He was not only the wisest man who ever lived but the richest one as well during his 40-year rulership of Israel. His reign was blessed by God with peace and tranquility, which was never known before. With his gift of wisdom, he achieved a great deal during his 40 years as king of Israel, including the building of the Holy Temple in Jerusalem. God will give wisdom to anyone who asks. *"If any of you lacks wisdom, let him ask God, who gives generously to all without reproach, and it will be given him"* **(James 1:5 ESV).**

An investment in knowledge pays the best dividends. Second chances are often second opportunities to accomplish your goals. Wounds heal, but scars remain as a reminder of how far you've come. Sometimes we expect too much from other people and not enough from ourselves. We need to step back to see the bigger picture. Have no regrets; whatever happens, is either a blessing or a lesson. Find out what your passion for life is and be the best you can at whatever you do.

No devil can stop God's plan for your life. He will try, but God will totally defeat all evil that comes against you. You cannot succeed alone; that's why every relationship in your life should be wisely selected. Only seek out those who add value to your life. Avoid small-minded thinking people that discourage your growth. Forgive and forget and move on. Sadness passes away, as do all emotions. They shift all the time. Be patient, and the tide will turn, and the light of the sun will appear. The paradox of transformation reveals, *"Anyone who loves their life will lose it, while anyone who hates their life in this world will keep it for eternal life"* (John 12:25 NIV).

If you trust in the Lord, He will give His angels charge over you and protect you against terror, pestilence, harm, disaster, and every demonic attack. *"If you say, 'The Lord is my refuge,' and you make the Most High your dwelling, no harm will overtake you, no disaster will come near your tent"* **(Psalm 91:9-10 NIV).**

Chapter 19
DEAL WISELY WITH YOUR PURPOSE IN LIFE

One must cease self-focusing in order to become more aware of life outside of one's self. This will broaden your scope of discovery and cause you to abandon self-consciousness. Cease fighting within yourself with negative thoughts, and fear will lose its power over you. Stop trying so hard to be heard. You'll find your true voice will be listened to by others with your integrity, upright behavior, and positive actions. Then, your opinions and sound reasoning will manifest a genuine voice and acceptance. Resist whatever doesn't make sense to your intellect. Pride and egos need to surrender to the divine epiphany that is clothed in wisdom, inspiration, and understanding.

When an enemy surfaces in your life and finds a group of witnesses to testify against you falsely, rest assured, God is the keeper of your soul. You shall not be moved by such false talebearing, but will prevail over these false witnesses. Know that God is greater than them all. He will always support you through any and all such vile attacks. God has compassion for all the trials and tribulations we go through. When His only begotten son, Jesus, was dying on the cross, God was so deeply affected by watching him being nailed to the cross, that He turned his back for one brief moment. He was in total agony, seeing His only begotten son die a horrific and painful death. He felt his anguish and pain with every nail that went into His Son's hands and feet. He knew His Son's death was necessary to fulfill His promise of redemption for mankind to be saved from their sins. This is how much God loves and cares for us. Praise God for the cross! We who believe have the Blessed Assurance that we are eternally saved through the bloodshed sacrifice of Jesus. *"He took up our pain and bore our suffering, yet we considered Him punished by God, stricken by Him, and afflicted. But He was pierced for our transgressions, He was crushed for our iniquities; the punishment that brought us peace was on Him, and by His wounds we are healed"* (Isaiah 53:4-5 NIV).

Every one of us should affirm in our heart, that regardless of all the challenges we face in this life, we are going to persevere because God will fight all our battles for us with a victory. All we have to do is have faith in Him and obey His laws. Then, we are hardwired to win. Tell yourself the simple truth that since you are going to be persistent and not give up, you're bound to overcome all your current and future trials. Know this, ***"I can do all things through Christ who strengthens me"*** **(Philippians 4:13 NKJV);** ***"And we know that all things work together for good to those who love God, to those who are the called according to His purpose"*** **(Romans 8:28 NKJV).**

Many wonderful blessings come in the midst of our trials. Surround yourself with those who want you to succeed. They will see their own success over their trials as well. This is a double edge sword **whenever two or more gather together, in the name of Jesus, and ask for his help, miracles can and do happen!!!** *"For where two or three are gathered together in My name, I am there in the midst of them"* (Matthew 18:20 NKJV). Make a declaration of believing God for your miracle and watch the seed of your faith grow and materialize in your success and victory over all your trials and tribulations!

True success is not just money in the bank or degrees on the wall; it goes much further than that. Living out our purpose is a priority in everyone's life. King Solomon, the wisest man who ever lived, discovered the futility of life when it is lived only for this world. He gives these concluding remarks in the Book of Ecclesiastes as to man's main purpose in this life, *"Here is the conclusion of the matter: Fear God and keep His commandments, for this is the duty of all mankind. For God will bring every deed into judgment, including every hidden thing, whether it is good or evil"* **(Ecclesiastes 12:13-14 NIV).**

One day, after we take our last breath in this body and our next breath in eternity, we will stand before God in judgment. Therefore, we should fear God and obey him. This is the whole duty of man. The main purpose of man is to love God, do his will, and glorify-Him forever. We glorify God by fearing him and following his purpose and plan for our lives and keeping his commandments always in our hearts. This gives us lasting joy and the abundant life that God desires for each of us.

To fear God is to do the following: We must have the proper reverence and awe for God, so we do whatever is required of us to serve Him, *"God is greatly to be feared in the assembly of the saints, And to be held in reverence by all those around Him"* (Psalm 89:7 NKJV). Everyone should stand respectfully and fearfully before God and do His will without being influenced by people or wanting to earn the good opinion of others. Know that we don't have to give an account to anyone but God. Never should we act against His will or dishonor Him in any way. We must always act with love and respect and not misrepresent Him or His Word to the world! God demands this from those in His ministry. Man's whole duty is to love God with all our heart, with all our strength, and to keep His commandments, *"What does the Lord your God require of you, but to fear the Lord your God, to walk in His ways and to love Him, to serve the Lord your God with all your heart and with all your soul, and to keep the commandments of the Lord and His statutes which I command you today for your good?"* **(Deuteronomy 10:12-13 NKJV)**

We can contribute to the lives of others by giving them love, hope, faith, kindness, and respect. The return will be greater than any monetary investment. God is the one who sees our acts of love and kindness, then blesses us richly for them. Our good works are rewarded and stored up in heaven. Everyone should embrace the beautiful fact that God loves us unconditionally and is present with us always. When we become less of ourselves and live more in Christ, we become full of love, joy, peace, wisdom, and knowledge, which we need to share with others.

Jesus commissions us to be His witnesses of His Father's Gospel to the world. His anointing empowers us to go forward and proclaim the Gospel of Jesus Christ. When the Lord speaks a word into our lives, it is like a seed that sprouts and germinates. Jesus promises every believer protection from their enemies. David, the psalmist, said, *"My times are in Your hand; Deliver me from the hand of my enemies, And from those who persecute me"* (Psalm 31:15 NKJV). God loves and cares for us! What He will do for one He will do for everyone. **GOD IS NO RESPECTOR OF PERSONS! WE ARE ALL EQUAL IN THE EYES OF GOD! HE DOES NOT SHOW FAVORITISM! ALL LIVES MATTER TO GOD!** (Acts 10:34)

Reaching your true potential is neither accessed nor realized apart from encountering life's challenges. The vitality of a dream for your future that lies dormant is awakened by the possibility of its death. Faith requires a fight and a good one at that. The fight is sometimes of considerable length involving our encounter of a strong opponent. Without resistance, there is no development of sustained passion and perseverance. Neither pain nor hardship, neither illness nor turmoil, neither sadness nor hurt, can keep God's loving grace from you. **So, forge ahead through all adversities with your dreams and goals, knowing God will make you victorious in all your endeavors.**

The prerequisite to success is perseverance! The more you feel like giving up, the closer you are to your harvest and reaping all the benefits of your hard work. Even though you are tired, weary, and feel like everything is spinning out of control in your life, don't give up! Close the door on what is holding you back from your destiny; slam it shut and throw away the key. Keep your mind on what you are designed to do. If you know your purpose and assignment, you will not have time to focus on any matter other than the goal that God has already carved out for you with success.

Affirming God's grace and praying for others, motivates us not to have a victim's mentality. It is vitally important not to challenge unhealthy talk because it diminishes our positive actions. Instead, create the reality of all good things, which will come out of your mind and heart, because you are destined to be divinely fruitful. We are the likeness and image of God, his son Jesus and his Holy Spirit. In the Holy Trinity, we have wonderful attributes that include a sound mind that is set on the positive things in life. We have the Father's plan for our life. Everyone has the capacity for mercy, compassion, and intellect that includes the capacity for faith in Jesus. This gives all believers the indwelling of the Holy Spirit and the gift of being one with the Blessed Trinity. **LET'S ALL STAND TALL AND PRAISE OUR HEAVENLY FATHER FOR HE LOVES EACH AND EVERYONE UNCONDITIONALLY!**

Chapter 20
JESUS PROMISED THE HOLY SPIRIT TO HIS DISCIPLES

Before his ascension into heaven, Jesus promised his disciples another helper, the Holy Spirit, the third person of the Holy Trinity. *"I will ask the Father, and He will give you another advocate to help you and be with you forever — the Spirit of Truth. The world cannot accept Him, because it neither sees Him nor knows Him. But you know him, for He lives with you and will be in you. I will not leave you as orphans; I will come to you"* **(John 14:16-18 NIV).**

The very moment you accept Jesus as your Lord and Savior, the Holy Spirit immediately dwells within your heart and mind. The Holy Spirit is a gift that is bestowed without merit upon all who repent of their sins and give their life to Jesus. God gives his Holy Spirit as a universal gift to every Christian, including every sinning Christian who repents of their transgressions. (see 1Corinthians 6:19, John 7:37-39, Acts 11:17, Romans 5:5; 1 Corinthians 2:12; and 2 Corinthians 5:5). All non-believers, who have sinned against God's Ten Commandments and have refused to accept Jesus as atonement for their sins, are in an unsaved state. They do not have the promise of eternal salvation or the indwelling presence of the Holy Spirit. (see Romans 8:9, Acts 19:2-5, and Jude 19).

Two thousand years ago, the Holy Spirit was given to the Apostles, the Jews, and the followers of Christ, ten days after Jesus ascended into heaven, and fifty days after His resurrection. This event occurred during a celebration held during Pentecost, a Jewish festival held on the seventh Sunday after Easter. This celebration is also known as the "Feast of Weeks" or the "Feast of Fifty Days." The disciples were all gathered together in one place when suddenly a sound came from heaven like the rush of a mighty wind and filled the house where they were celebrating. *"Suddenly, a sound like the blowing of a violent wind came from heaven and filled the whole house where they were sitting. They saw what seemed to be tongues of fire that separated and came to rest on each of them. All of them were filled with the Holy Spirit and began to speak in other tongues as the Spirit enabled them. Now there were staying in Jerusalem God-fearing Jews from every nation under heaven. When they heard this sound, a crowd came together in bewilderment, because each one heard their own language being spoken. Utterly amazed, they asked: "Aren't all these who are speaking Galileans?"* **(Acts 2:2-7 NIV)**

The moment the Holy Spirit appeared like tongues of fire resting on each one of them, they began to speak in other tongues as the Spirit gave them utterance. Today believers have this same power, with the indwelling of the Holy Spirit, who dispenses His gifts as they are needed.

THIS IS WHAT THE HOLY SPIRIT DOES FOR EACH ONE OF US:

HE CONVICTS US OF SIN

> *"But very truly I tell you, it is for your good that I am going away. Unless I go away, the Advocate will not come to you; but if I go, I will send Him to you. When He comes, He will prove the world to be in the wrong about sin and righteousness and judgment:*

about sin, because people do not believe in Me; about righteousness, because I am going to the Father, where you can see me no longer; and about judgment, because the prince of this world now stands condemned" (John 16:7-11 NIV).

HE TEACHES GOD'S WORD

"We do, however, speak a message of wisdom among the mature, but not the wisdom of this age or of the rulers of this age, who are coming to nothing. No, we declare God's wisdom, a mystery that has been hidden and that God destined for our glory before time began. None of the rulers of this age understood it, for if they had, they would not have crucified the Lord of glory. However, as it is written: 'What no eye has seen, what no ear has heard, and what no human mind has conceived' the things God has prepared for those who love him. These are the things God has revealed to us by his Spirit. The Spirit searches all things, even the deep things of God. For who knows a person's thoughts except their own spirit within them? In the same way no one knows the thoughts of God except the Spirit of God. What we have received is not the spirit of the world, but the Spirit who is from God, so that we may understand what God has freely given us. This is what we speak, not in words taught us by human wisdom but in words taught by the Spirit, explaining spiritual realities with Spirit-taught words. The person without the Spirit does not accept the things that come from the Spirit of God but considers them foolishness, and cannot understand them because they are discerned only through the Spirit. The person with the Spirit makes judgments about all things, but such a person is not subject to merely human judgments, for, 'Who has known the mind of the Lord so as to instruct him?' But we have the mind of Christ" (1 Corinthians 2:6-16 NIV).

HE DRAWS US TO JESUS

"He will glorify me because it is from me that he will receive what he will make known to you" (John 16:14 NIV).

HE CONCEIVED JESUS IN THE WOMB OF A VIRGIN

"An angel of the Lord appeared to him in a dream and said, 'Joseph son of David, do not be afraid to take Mary home as your wife, because what is conceived in her is from the Holy Spirit. She will give birth to a son, and you are to give him the name Jesus, because He will save His people from their sins'" (Matthew 1:20-21 NIV).)

HE WAS WITH JESUS DURING HIS BAPTISM.

"John saw Jesus coming toward him and said, 'Look, the Lamb of God, who takes away the sin of the world! This is the one I meant when I said, 'A man who comes after me has surpassed me because he was before me.' I myself did not know him, but the reason I came baptizing with water was that he might be revealed to Israel.'" Then John gave this testimony: 'I saw the Spirit come down from heaven as a dove and remain on him'" (John 1:29-32 NIV).

From heaven, the Lord Jesus Christ baptized his church with his Holy Spirit, and the church of Jesus Christ was born. In that very moment, when believers in Jesus Christ received the Holy Spirit, they were no longer under the condemnation of the flesh but became the sons of God. *"Therefore, brethren, we are debtors—not to the flesh, to live according to the flesh. For if you live according to the flesh you will die; but if by the Spirit you put to death the deeds of the body, you will live"* (Romans 8:12-13 NKJV). **The Holy Spirit is the only person you are required to please your entire lifetime!**

THERE ARE NINE GIFTS OF THE HOLY SPIRIT

"Now to each one the manifestation of the Spirit is given for the common good. To one there is given through the Spirit a message of wisdom, to another a message of knowledge by means of the same Spirit, to another faith by the same Spirit, to another gifts of healing by that one Spirit, to another miraculous powers, to another prophecy, to another distinguishing between spirits, to another speaking in different kinds of tongues, and to still another the interpretation of tongues. All these are the work of one and the same Spirit, and he distributes them to each one, just as he determines" (1 Corinthians 12:7-11 NIV).

THE NINE GIFTS ARE DEFINED AS FOLLOWS:

1. A Message of Wisdom

A message of wisdom is a supernatural revelation, or insight into the divine will and purpose, often given by the Spirit to solve perplexing problems and situations.

2. A Message of Knowledge

A word of knowledge is a supernatural revelation of divine knowledge or insight in the divine mind, will, or plan, to know things that could not be known of oneself.

3. A Gift of Faith

A gift of faith is a supernatural ability to believe God without human doubt, unbelief, or reasonings.

4. A Gift of Healing

The gift of healing of all manner of sickness by supernatural power, without human aid or medicine.

5. A Gift of Miraculous Powers

A gift of miraculous power is the supernatural ability to intervene in the ordinary course of nature and to counteract natural laws if necessary.

6. A Gift of Prophecy

Prophecy is the supernatural utterance in the native tongue. It is a miracle of divine utterance, not conceived by human thought or reasoning. It includes speaking unto men for edification, exhortation, and comfort.

7. A Gift of Discerning of Spirits

This is a supernatural revelation or insight into the realm of spirits to detect them and their plans and to read the minds of men.

8. A Gift of Speaking in Tongues

The gift of speaking in tongues is the supernatural utterance in other languages that are not known to the speaker.

9. The Gift of Interpretation of Tongues

The gift of interpretation of tongues the supernatural ability to interpret, in the native tongue, what is being uttered in other languages, not known by the one who interprets by the spirit.

The Holy Spirit's work is to exalt Christ and to focus our salvation through him. God gives every believer the Holy Spirit so we can be totally under His influence in every aspect of our lives, as to what we should say, what we should do, and what we should think. *"Each of you should use whatever gift you have received to serve others, as faithful stewards of God's grace in its various forms"* **(1 Peter 4:10 NIV).**

Chapter 21
OUR ALMIGHTY GOD IS A SPIRIT

JOHN 4:24

Jesus said, *"God is a Spirit: and they that worship him must worship him in spirit and in truth"* (John 4:24 KJV). God has always existed. No one created him. He does not have a human body, like His Son, Jesus, who came to earth in human form. In His pre-human state, Jesus is the eternal God the son. Upon His virgin birth, as God's Messiah to mankind, he is called Immanuel, *"'The virgin will conceive and give birth to a son, and they will call him Immanuel' (which means 'God with us')"* (Matthew 1:23 NIV).

Some scriptures speak of God having body parts: for example, arms and ears, *"Surely **the arm of the Lord** is not too short to save, nor **His ear** too dull to hear"* (Isaiah 59:1 NIV), or eyes, *"For the **eyes of the Lord** range throughout the earth to strengthen those whose hearts are fully committed to Him"* (2 Chronicles 16:9 NIV), or a mouth, *"It is written: 'Man shall not live on bread alone, but on every word that comes from the mouth of God'"* (Matthew 4:4 NIV).

All of these verses are a way of describing God's Spirit. He does possess these body parts, but not with a flesh-and-blood body like Jesus. God is invisible, yet can be seen face-to-face as He was when

He spoke to Moses. We are the likeness and image of God, and in flesh-and-blood form like Jesus. Our bodies are the Temple of God, yet we cannot see Him physically, because He dwells in us in spirit and truth (see John 14:17). *"The Son is the image of the invisible God, the firstborn over all creation"* (Colossians 1:15 NIV).

God is a **living spiritual being**, who we can know personally. *"My soul yearns, even faints, for the courts of the Lord; my heart and my flesh cry out for the living God"* (Psalm 84:2 NIV). **God is infinite** and not limited to a physical body. He is omnipresent, and can be in all places at the same time, and can dwell in everyone at the same time. He has no dimensional restrictions. No one created God. He created all things through His only begotten Son, Jesus, ***"For by Him all things were created, in heaven and on earth, visible and invisible, whether thrones or dominions or rulers or authorities—all things were created through Him and for Him"*** **(Colossians 1:16 ESV).**

Visions of God were given to both Apostle John and the Prophet Ezekiel, which depict the splendors of the most high God, Jehovah, and His awe-inspiring beauty, peace, and serenity. *"A throne set in heaven, and One sat on the throne. And He who sat there was like a jasper and a sardius stone in appearance; and there was a rainbow around the throne, in appearance like an emerald"* (Revelation 4:2-3 NKJV), *"Like the appearance of a rainbow in a cloud on a rainy day, so was the appearance of the brightness all around it. This was the appearance of the likeness of the glory of the Lord"* (Ezekiel 1:28 NKJV).

Our supreme, almighty, and merciful God invites everyone to approach Him in prayer in His throne room of grace. When we do this, he listens to all our prayers and supplications, ***"You who answer prayer, to you all people will come"*** **(Psalm 65:2 NIV).** ***"You are enthroned as the Holy One; you are the one Israel praises"*** **(Psalm 22:3 NIV).**

BIBLICAL NAMES OF GOD'S HOLY SPIRIT:

Breath of the Almighty

*"The Spirit of God has made me, And the **Breath of the Almighty** gives me life"* (Job 33:4 NKJV).

Counselor and Comforter

*"I will ask the Father, and he will give you another **Counselor** to be with you forever"* (John 14:16 EHV).

*"But the **Comforter**, which is the Holy Ghost, whom the Father will send in my name, he shall teach you all things, and bring all things to your remembrance, whatsoever I have said unto you"* (John 14:26 KJV).

Eternal Spirit

*"How much more, then, will the blood of Christ, who through the **Eternal Spirit** offered himself unblemished to God, cleanse our consciences from acts that lead to death, so that we may serve the living God!"* (Hebrews 9:14 NIV)

Free Spirit

*"Restore unto me the joy of thy salvation; and uphold me with thy **Free Spirit**"* (Psalm 51:12 NIV).

God (the third person of the trinity)

*"But Peter said, "Ananias, why has Satan filled your heart to lie to the **Holy Spirit** and keep back part of the price of the land for yourself? While it remained, was it not your own? And after it was sold, was it not in your own control? Why have you conceived this thing in your heart? You have not lied to men but to **God**"* (Acts 5:3-4 NKJV).

Good Spirit

*"You gave your **Good Spirit** to instruct them. You did not with-hold your manna from their mouths, and you gave them water for their thirst"* (Nehemiah 9:20 NIV).

Holy Spirit

*"In Him you also trusted, after you heard the word of truth, the gospel of your salvation; in whom also, having believed, you were sealed with the **Holy Spirit** of promise"* (Ephesians 1:13 NKJV).

Lord

*"Now the **Lord** is the Spirit; and where the Spirit of the Lord is, there is liberty"* (2 Corinthians 3:17 NKJV).

The Holy Ghost

*"And the angel answered and said unto her, **The Holy** Ghost shall come upon thee, and the Power of the Highest shall over-shadow thee: therefore also that holy thing which shall be born of thee shall be called the Son of God"* (Luke 1:35 KJV).

Spirit

*"Then Jesus was led by the **Spirit** into the wilderness to be tempted by the devil"* (Matthew 4:1 NIV).

*"**The Spirit** clearly says that in later times some will abandon the faith and follow deceiving spirits and things taught by de-mons"* (1 Timothy 4:1 NIV).

Spirit of Adoption

*"For you did not receive the spirit of bondage again to fear, but you received the **Spirit of Adoption** by whom we cry out, 'Abba, Father'"* (Romans 8:15 NKJV).

Spirit of Burning

*"When the Lord has washed away the filth of the daughters of Zion, and purged the blood of Jerusalem from her midst, by the spirit of judgment and by the **Spirit of Burning**"* (Isaiah 4:4 NKJV).

Spirit of Christ

*"But you are not in the flesh but in the Spirit, if indeed the Spirit of God dwells in you. Now if anyone does not have the **Spirit of Christ**, he is not His"* (Romans 8:9 NKJV).

Spirit of Counsel

*"The Spirit of the Lord will rest on him—the Spirit of wisdom and of understanding, the **Spirit of Counsel** and of might, the Spirit of the knowledge and fear of the Lord"* (Isaiah 11:2 NIV).

Spirit of Glory

*"If you are insulted because of the name of Christ, you are blessed, for the **Spirit of Glory** and of God rests on you"* (Isaiah 11:2 NIV).

Spirit of God (Triune God)

*"For what man knows the things of a man except the spirit of the man which is in him? Even so no one knows the things of God except the **Spirit of God**"* (1 Corinthians 2:11 NKJV).

Spirit of Grace

*"How much more severely do you think someone deserves to be punished who has trampled the Son of God underfoot, who has treated as an unholy thing the blood of the covenant that sanctified them, and who has insulted the **Spirit of Grace?**"* (1 Corinthians 2:11 NIV)

Spirit of Judgment (the Spirit convicts us of sin)

*"The Lord will wash away the filth of the women of Zion; he will cleanse the bloodstains from Jerusalem by a **Spirit of Judgment** and a spirit of fire"* (1 Corinthians 2:11 NIV).

Spirit of Knowledge and Fear of the Lord

*"The Spirit of the Lord shall rest upon Him, The Spirit of wisdom and understanding, The Spirit of counsel and might, **The Spirit of Knowledge and of the Fear of the Lord**"* (Isaiah 11:2 NKJV).

Spirit of Life

*"For the law of the **Spirit of Life** in Christ Jesus has made me free from the law of sin and death"* (Romans 8:2 NKJV).

Spirit of Might

*"The Spirit of the Lord shall rest upon Him, The Spirit of wisdom and understanding, The **Spirit of Counsel and Might**, The Spirit of knowledge and of the fear of the Lord"* (Isaiah 11:2 NKJV).

Spirit of Prophecy

"At this I fell at his feet to worship him. But he said to me, 'Don't

*do that! I am a fellow servant with you and with your brothers and sisters who hold to the testimony of Jesus. Worship God! For it is the **Spirit of Prophecy** who bears testimony to Jesus'"* (Revelation 19:10 NIV).

Spirit of Revelation

*"The Spirit of the Lord shall rest upon Him, **The Spirit of Wisdom and Understanding**, The Spirit of counsel and might, The Spirit of Knowledge and of the fear of the Lord"* (Isaiah 11:2 NKJV).

Spirit of the Father

*"For it is not you who speak, but the **Spirit of your** Father who speaks in you"* (Matthew 10:20 NKJV).

Spirit of Knowledge and Fear of the Lord

*"The Spirit of the Lord shall rest upon Him, The Spirit of wisdom and understanding, The Spirit of counsel and might, **The Spirit of Knowledge and of the Fear of the Lord**"* (Isaiah 11:2 NKJV).

Spirit of the Living God

*"Clearly you are an epistle of Christ, ministered by us, written not with ink but by the **Spirit of the Living God**, not on tablets of stone but on tablets of flesh, that is, of the heart"* (2 Corinthians 3:3 NKJV).

Spirit of the Lord

*"Peter said to her, 'How could you conspire to test the **Spirit of the Lord**? Listen! The feet of the men who buried your husband are at the door, and they will carry you out also'"* (Acts 5:9 NIV).

Spirit of the Son

*"And because you are sons, God has sent forth the **Spirit of His Son** into your hearts, crying out, 'Abba, Father!'"* (Galatians 4:6 NKJV)

Spirit of Truth

*"The **Spirit of Truth**, whom the world cannot receive, because it neither sees Him nor knows Him; but you know Him, for He dwells with you and will be in you"* (John 14:17 NKJV).

Spirit of Understanding

*"The Spirit of the Lord shall rest upon Him, **The Spirit of Wisdom and Understanding**, The Spirit of counsel and might, The Spirit of Knowledge and of the fear of the Lord"* (Isaiah 11:2 NKJV).

Spirit of Wisdom

*"that the God of our Lord Jesus Christ, the Father of glory, may give to you the **Spirit of Wisdom** and revelation in the knowledge of Him"* (Ephesians 1:17 NKJV).

Spirit of Yahweh

*"And the **Spirit of Yahweh** shall rest on him—a spirit of wisdom and understanding, a spirit of counsel and might, a spirit of knowledge and the fear of Yahweh"* (Isaiah 11:2 LEB).

Chapter 22

THE UNFORGIVABLE SIN THAT GRIEVES THE HOLY SPIRIT

There is an unforgivable sin, and that is blasphemy against the Holy Spirit. As stated in the synoptic gospels:

"Therefore I say to you, every sin and blasphemy will be forgiven men, but the blasphemy against the Spirit will not be forgiven men. Anyone who speaks a word against the Son of Man, it will be forgiven him; but whoever speaks against the Holy Spirit, it will not be forgiven him, either in this age or in the age to come" (Matthew 12:31-32 NKJV).

"Assuredly, I say to you, all sins will be forgiven the sons of men, and whatever blasphemies they may utter; but he who blasphemes against the Holy Spirit never has forgiveness, but is subject to eternal condemnation" (Mark 3:28-29 NKJV). *"*

"And anyone who speaks a word against the Son of Man, it will be forgiven him; but to him who blasphemes against the Holy Spirit, it will not be forgiven" (Luke 12:10 NKJV).

Anyone who speaks a word against the Son of Man will be forgiven, but if one rejects Jesus as atonement for their sins, they condemn their soul into the fires of hell. Jesus describes hell as a place of torment, where the fire is not quenched. *"If your hand causes you to sin, cut it off. It is better for you to enter into life maimed, rather than having two hands, to go to hell, into the fire that shall never be quenched"* (Mark 9:43 NKJV). As protection against Satan, we are told to put on the whole Armor of God. *"Put on the whole armor of God, that you may be able to stand against the [a]wiles of the devil"* (Ephesians 6:11 NKJV).). This will extinguish the power of Satan's fiery darts. When we go against the prompting of the Holy Spirit and do what we know is wrong, we reject the spirit: *"Do not quench the Spirit. Do not treat prophecies with contempt"* (1 Thessalonians 5:19-20 NIV). **This is an unforgivable sin because we are saying the Holy Spirit's witness about Jesus is a lie. Jesus was God in human flesh, and God's appointed means of salvation.** *"No one has ever seen God, but the one and only Son, who is himself God and is in closest relationship with the Father, has made him known"* (John 1:18 NIV). **By His death and resurrection, Jesus provided the way for us to be forgiven and cleansed of all our sins.**

It is important to understand the person of the Holy Spirit. The Holy Spirit is not only God, but He has a will, a personality, and can even be offended! We are told we should not grieve the Holy Spirit. *"Do not grieve the Holy Spirit of God, by whom you were sealed for the day of redemption"* (Ephesians 4:30 NKJV). To grieve means to make sad. It means to cause sorrow, pain, or distress. We grieve the spirit by living an unholy and sinful life and not following God's Commandments, which includes:

> **Lying,** *"Therefore, putting away lying, 'Let each one of you speak truth with his neighbor,' for we are members of one another"* (Ephesians 4:25 NKJV).

> **Being angry.** *"In your anger do not sin: Do not let the sun go down while you are still angry, and do not give the devil a foothold"* (Ephesians 4:26-27 NIV),.

Stealing, *"Anyone who has been stealing must steal no longer, but must work, doing something useful with their own hands, that they may have something to share with those in need"* (Ephesians 4:28 NIV).

Cursing, *"Watch your talk! No bad words should be coming from your mouth. Say what is good. Your words should help others grow as Christians"* (Ephesians 4:29 NLV).

Being bitter, *"Get rid of all bitterness, rage and anger, brawling and slander, along with every form of malice"* (Ephesians 4:31 NIV).

Being unforgiving, *"And be kind to one another, tender-hearted, forgiving one another, even as God in Christ forgave you"* (Ephesians 4:32 NKJV).

Being sexually immoral, *"Among you there must not be even a hint of sexual immorality, or of any kind of impurity, or of greed, because these are improper for God's holy people"* (Ephesians 5:3 NIV).

To grieve the Holy Spirit is to act in a sinful manner, in thought, word, or deed. The Holy Spirit was present before the creation of the universe, and through His power, everything was made by and for Jesus Christ, by God the Father who created all the matter for Jesus to create everything.

The Holy Spirit convicts us of sin. (see John 16:7-11). He teaches us the truth and leads us to Christ so we can be changed and be more like Jesus. (see 1 Corinthians 2:6-16). He does all of this so that on the day of our redemption, we can be changed from this life into the next. He exposes our guilt, reveals our sin, speaks the truth, and directs us to Jesus. He reveals as He did to the Apostles that Jesus Christ is the way, the truth, and the life. **The Holy Spirit**

speaks for the Father and the Son that the true meaning of our salvation is to accept Jesus as our Lord and Savior and repent of our sins!

The entire Bible was written under the inspiration of the Holy Spirit. The writers of the New Testament included the Apostles and those under their authority. The Bible is the Holy Spirit's book! His role is to serve and exalt Christ. *"He will glorify Me because it is from Me that He will receive what He will make known to you"* **(John 16:14 NIV).** All three persons of the Holy Trinity are fully God. In their divine nature, the Son makes known the Father, and the Spirit glorifies the Son.

The Holy Spirit helps us to make the right decisions in our walk-through life. In Chapter 20, we spoke of the nine gifts of the Holy Spirit, which he dispenses in a believer's life when needed. They are (1) A message of wisdom to solve our problems. (2) A word of knowledge, which is divine knowledge. (3) The gift of faith, which is the supernatural ability to believe God without human doubt, unbelief, and reasonings. (4) The gift of healing, which is healing sickness by supernatural power without the aid of medicine or man. (5) The gift of working of miracles, which is a supernatural power to counteract natural laws. (6) The gift of prophecy, which includes speaking to men in order to edify, exhort, and comfort. (7) The gift of discerning of spirits, which is a supernatural revelation into the realm of spirits. (8) Speaking in tongues, a language that is not known to the speaker. (9) The interpretation of tongues, which is the supernatural ability to interpret the native tongue that is not known to the interpreter. These gifts will be given to every believer as needed in their life until Christ returns.

If we ignore the prompting of the Holy Spirit and choose the wrong door to go through, we will look back with regret. The one door that does not lead to regret is the door to our Lord and Savior,

Jesus Christ. Through Him, we receive any one or all of the nine gifts of the Holy Spirit as needed, and God's saving grace to have all our sins forgiven, past, present, and future. God gave to the world the life of His only begotten Son, Jesus, to be the atonement for mankind's sins. Our salvation was sealed when Jesus went willingly to the Cross of Calvary, where His hands and feet were cruelly nailed to the Cross, and He died in extreme suffering, torment, and writhing pain. He took upon Himself our just punishment for all our sins. The final blow to His dead body was not only from those who mocked his Godly sacrifice but from a soldier who thrust a spear through his side where blood and water gushed out. *"One of the soldiers pierced His side with a spear, and immediately blood and water came out"* (John 19:34 NKJV).

Eternal salvation was guaranteed by Jesus' death on the cross, for all who accepted Him as their Lord and Savior and repented of their sins. Upon his second coming, all the believers will receive a brand-new incorruptible body and have everlasting joy and happiness with their saved loved ones. What a joyous reunion that will be!

We must keep our faith in God, His Word, and His Son, Jesus. Regardless of what one goes through, God will defeat the wiles of Satan and all his demons and utterly destroy their influence over the redeemed. Having a positive mindset on God's Word will support your faith well, regardless of what trials you go through. Know that God is the light to direct your path and that He will never leave or forsake you. ***"Be strong and of good courage, do not fear nor be afraid of them; for the Lord your God, He is the One who goes with you. He will not leave you nor forsake you"*** **(Deuteronomy 31:6 NKJV).**

Changes are certain to happen in everyone's life. Know that the power of the Holy Spirit dwells within us and gives His divine gifts freely to every believer as we go through life with all our inevitable challenges. His Holy Intercession will give victory to all our God-given endeavors. Being in Christ means you dwell less in yourself and more and more in Him. This is what life's lessons are all about. To increase ones' faith, so we can reap the benefits of having His ways prevail over our ways of doing things. **Never forget that, in Christ, we are overcomers from all our adversities. God equips and fortifies us, as we go through life's trials, tribulations, and spiritual warfare. He develops our character as we grow and mature in the Spirit. With God, no problem is too great. He gives divine intervention to every believer.**

Chapter 23
SATAN'S DIABOLICAL PLAN FOR YOUR LIFE IS DEATH AND DESTRUCTION

Satan's plan for your life is to cause death and destruction. If you follow him, he will lead you to the end of your rope and towards your ETERNAL DEMISE. Those who walk by faith need not fear his demonic attacks because no evil will come upon those who put their trust and faith in God. He will fight all your battles and squash every demonic attack. His almighty power gives victory to those who remain steadfast in their faith. Every battle offers challenges, but the seasoned warrior is one who has been tempered and balanced by the seasons of uncertainties. They have experienced and endured and overcome all their trials. When they are feeling out of sync, out of step, or out of touch, this only deepens and widens their effectiveness because God takes over their battle completely. Never fear or be afraid of anything, because if you walk by faith and not by sight, the Lord is always present for those who believe in Him. We must strive to pursue **excessive faith**. In so doing, we have God's supernatural intervention and His victory over all our battles. *"And we know that all things work together for good to them that love God, to them who are the called according to his purpose"* (Romans 8:28 KJV. Remember, all things work for the good for those who love God.

Tomorrow belongs to no one. If you plan on something supernatural and keep the faith, it will happen in your life. Plant every seed and wait in expectation, then watch it grow into fruition. Speak proficiently over your days as you enter into tomorrow morning, and prophesize daily all good things for your life. You must speak the events that you want to occur in your life. Every day is a blessing from God. Believe this, and expect good things to happen, and they will. Embrace life as a gift, and you will never be disappointed. In the name of Jesus, I claim this knowledge will be embraced by everyone. No one who ever gave his best regretted it. You will only achieve success when you make an effort. Be courageous in life's journey, no matter where it leads you. Be patient as you go through your adversities, knowing God will defeat all your enemies. *"'No weapon formed against you shall prosper, And every tongue which rises against you in judgment You shall condemn. This is the heritage of the servants of the Lord, And their righteousness is from Me,' Says the Lord"* **(Isaiah 54:17 NKJV).**

Do not rush or hurry through life, but savor every moment with thanksgiving, and know that God is in control! The ultimate value of life depends upon our awareness and the power of deep contemplation and faith. Stay the course and wait for God to speak in regard to the direction he wants you to take. Stand ready with the breastplate of righteousness, and with your feet grounded in truth. Every believer in Jesus Christ has all the flaming arrows of salvation, the full armor of God, and the sword of the spirit, which is the Word of God. This equips us to fight every single battle and every demonic attack. The faithful shall be glad in the Lord when they trust in Him only. We are the workmanship of God, which means no one can define our personality, determine our potential, or defeat our purpose. Only God can and does control our journey through life and our destiny. There is a war going on, and your mind is the battlefield. The good news is that God is fighting your battles for you and is on your side. Heaven has high hopes for you if you align yourself with God's will. There is no stopping those who do this.

Chapter 24
SATAN'S WARFARE IS FOR CONTROL OF YOUR MIND

The mind resides in a living working brain. It is part of the nervous system which runs the entire body. The nervous system is made up of large cells called neurons. According to neuroscience, **"the mind is the brain in action. The mind is the state when the brain is alive and at work. When the brain is dead, the mind cannot function."** The Bible confirms that the mind only exists in the brain while we are alive. *"His spirit departs, he returns to the earth; In that very day his thoughts perish"* (Psalm 146:4 NASB). Once we take our last breath, the spirit goes back to God who gave it. *"Then the dust will return to the earth as it was, And the spirit will return to God who gave it"* (Ecclesiastes 12:7 NKJV).

While we have God's breath of life in us, we should use our minds to serve him. *"Then the Lord God formed a man from the dust of the ground and breathed into his nostrils the breath of life, and the man became a living being"* (Genesis 2:7 NIV). Our thoughts are vitally important to our living this life successfully. They have the power to mold our actions and influence our lives and the lives of those around us. We each have the choice of what we want to meditate on. **Toxic thoughts, such as stress, worry, fear, anger, and unforgiveness, cause chemicals to be released into the brain**. This can cause a loss of sleep, physical and mental illness, poor performance at any job we undertake and can be costly and debilitating. We must guard our minds with only thoughts that keep our mind in an attitude of faith, praise, thanksgiving, and the knowledge of God's love and salvation through His Son Jesus. Then, we can overcome any and all trials and be delivered from all demonic attacks. Satan and his demons cannot stand to be in the presence of Christians praying and praising God. Praying keeps the devil away. This is why the bible counsels us to *"Pray without ceasing, in everything give thanks; for this is the will of God in Christ Jesus for you"* (1 Thessalonians 5:17-18 NKJV).

We must stay steadfast in our faith. It is God, who steers us into paths of righteousness, and fights our battles for us against Satan and all our enemies. With His Blessed Assurance of Victory. He also counsels us to think of things that are true, honest, just, pure, lovely, or of good report; and of virtue and anything praiseworthy. *"Whatever things are true, whatever things are noble, whatever things are just, whatever things are pure, whatever things are lovely, whatever things are of good report, if there is any virtue and if there is anything praiseworthy—meditate on these things"* (Philippians 4:8 NKJV).The Bible warns, *"Do not be conformed to this world, but be transformed by the renewing of your mind, that you may prove what is that good and acceptable and perfect will of God"* (Romans 12:2 NKJV).

Satan cannot read, penetrate, or violate the sanctity of our mind unless we open the door to him. Those who open the door to Satan will find he holds their minds and lives captive with his projected evil thoughts. We need only good, spirit-filled thoughts that will direct our lives towards God, our Savior, Jesus Christ, and our eternal destination in the Kingdom of God. Satan will only lead those who follow him to death and destruction. His goal is to instill his rebellious thoughts against God and his Laws and to control our life to sin and be eternally damned. Guard your mind like you would the privacy of your home. You need to be careful who you allow into your home, as well as what thoughts you allow into your mind. We must practice this daily, by using discipline and allowing God's Holy Spirit to direct us in all ways. He dwells in every believer and uses His spiritual gifts to support us in our walk through this life. He gives us only positive thoughts of peace, joy, and confidence to go forward with faith and love for God, Jesus, and our fellow man.

Controlling our thoughts must be learned and practiced daily. When we act upon Satan's projected thoughts, that are not only negative but totally evil, they will steer us towards non-productive and sinful acts. Satan's goal is to take control of our thinking and actions through lies and deceptions. Undisciplined thoughts are an easy target for Satan to direct one's life towards evil and to put chains of bondage on their life. If we do not bring our thoughts into captivity to the obedience of Christ, Satan will infiltrate his evil and vile thoughts in our mind to dismantle our lives to cause utter ruin and destruction. Apostle Paul said we are in a spiritual war and that we should take every thought captive and subject all thinking to Jesus Christ. *"We demolish arguments and every pretension that sets itself up against the knowledge of God, and we take captive every thought to make it obedient to Christ"* **(2 Corinthians 10:5 NIV).**

God's perfect love for us casts out any and all fear from our lives. *"There is no fear in love; but perfect love casts out fear, because fear involves torment. But he who fears has not been made perfect in love"* (1 John 4:18 NKJV). Fear is another tool of the devil that can rule over us and keep us from fulfilling God's plan for our life. His goal is to take away the peace that Jesus gives to each of us and replace it with fear. Satan wants us to lose faith in God and our salvation through Jesus Christ. Fear enters our mind as a thought. *"For as he thinks in his heart, so is he"* **(Proverbs 23:7 NKJV).** This is why meditating on God's Word is vitally important and healthy for our minds. We must always praise God for the confirmation in His Word for our eternal salvation through Jesus Christ. We are counseled to do the good works that God preordained us to do. *"For we are God's handiwork, created in Christ Jesus to do good works, which God prepared in advance for us to do"* **(Ephesians 2:10 NIV).**

Satan controls the hearts and minds of those who reject the wisdom and knowledge of God. The world today is positive proof of the impact of his projected evil thoughts on those people and their lives. **Satan possesses more souls today than those who are saved through the blood of Jesus.** *"Though the number of the sons of Israel be as the sand of the sea, only a remnant of them will be saved"* (Romans 9:27 ESV). We must guard our minds with only positive, wholesome, and constructive thoughts, and not allow Satan's vile temptations to cause us to sin. Once sin enters our life, it makes us guilt-ridden, afraid, and ashamed. This is why our Sovereign God, who knows our thoughts and our weaknesses, wants to save us from Satan's evil acts. There is demonic spiritual warfare going on for the souls of men. This is why God has given His angels charge over each one of us, to protect and guide us from all demonic spirits. The Bible says, "Are not all angels ministering spirits sent to serve those who will inherit salvation?" (Hebrews 1:14)

God's Laws were created from His mind and heart because He loves each and every one of us unconditionally, despite all our sins. He wants His Laws to guide and direct us towards how we treat each other and to honor and love Him. He knows we are not perfect. That's why he offered His Son Jesus to die on the Cross of Calvary, as atonement for all our sins, past, present, and future. All those who accept Him are forgiven and saved from their sins and eternal damnation. All those who reject Jesus as atonement for their sins, will die without being saved and have to pay, in the fires of hell, for their own sins. God takes no pleasure in an unrepentant sinner's rejection of His saving grace or their death. *"For I take no pleasure in the death of anyone, declares the Sovereign Lord. Repent and live!"* **(Ezekiel 18:32 NIV)**

SCRIPTURAL GUIDANCE TO GUARD YOUR THOUGHTS AND MIND:

Isaiah 26:3 ESV

"You keep him in perfect peace whose mind is stayed on you, because he trusts in you."

Psalm 94:11 ESV

"The Lord—knows the thoughts of man, that they are but a breath."

Psalm 139:23-24 ESV

"Search me, O God, and know my heart! Try me and know my thoughts! And see if there be any grievous way in me, and lead me in the way everlasting!"

Matthew 22:37 ESV

"And he said to him, 'you shall love the Lord your God with all your heart and with all your soul and with all your mind.'"

Mark 7:21-22 ESV

"For from within, out of the heart of man, come evil thoughts, sexual immorality, theft, murder, adultery, coveting, wickedness, deceit, sensuality, envy, slander, pride, foolishness."

Mark 12:30 ESV

"You shall love the Lord your God with all your heart and with all your soul and with all your mind and with all your strength."

Romans 7:23 ESV

"I see in my members another law waging war against the law of my mind and making me captive to the law of sin that dwells in my members."

Romans 7:25 ESV

"Thanks be to God through Jesus Christ our Lord! So then, I myself serve the Law of God with my mind, but with my flesh I serve the law of sin."

Romans 8:6 ESV

"For to set the mind on the flesh is death, but to set the mind on the Spirit is life and peace."

Romans 12:2 ESV

"Do not be conformed to this world, but be transformed by the renewal of your mind, that by testing you may discern what is the will of God, what is good and acceptable and perfect."

Romans 12:3 ESV

"For by the grace given to me I say to everyone among you not to think of himself more highly than he ought to think, but to think with sober judgment, each according to the measure of faith that God has assigned."

1 Corinthians 2:11 ESV

"For who knows a person's thoughts except the spirit of that person, which is in him? So also no one comprehends the thoughts of God except the Spirit of God."

1 Corinthians 2:16 ESV

"For who has understood the mind of the Lord so as to instruct him?' but we have the mind of Christ."

2 Corinthians 10:5 ESV

"We destroy arguments and every lofty opinion raised against the knowledge of God, and take every thought captive to obey Christ."

Ephesians 4:23 ESV

"And to be renewed in the spirit of your minds."

Philippians 2:5 ESV

"Have this mind among yourselves, which is yours in Christ Jesus."

Philippians 4:6-7 ESV

"Do not be anxious about anything, but in everything by prayer and supplication with thanksgiving let your requests be made known to God. And the peace of God, which surpasses all understanding, will guard your hearts and your minds in Christ Jesus."

Philippians 4:8-9 ESV

"Finally, brothers, whatever is true, whatever is honorable, whatever is just, whatever is pure, whatever is lovely, whatever is commendable, if there is any excellence, if there is anything worthy of praise, think about these things. What you have learned and received and heard and seen in me—practice these things, and the god of peace will be with you.

Colossians 3:2 ESV

"Set your minds on things that are above, not on things that are on earth."

James 1:8 ESV

"A double-minded man is unstable in all his ways."

1 Peter 1:13 ESV

"Therefore, preparing your minds for action, and being sober-minded, set your hope fully on the grace that will be brought to you at the revelation of Jesus Christ."

These scriptures confirm that when you renew your mind with good thoughts, you produce positive energy, feelings, and emotions. **It does matter what we think because it affects our mind, body, and spirit. Only allow good thoughts in your mind, and take the bad thoughts captive. Keep your faith and mind fixed on God. Then your life will be blessed beyond measure, and the desires of your heart will materialize.**

Chapter 25
FAITH-FILLED CHRISTIANS CAN SOAR LIKE EAGLES

We must have an attitude of believing we can do anything that God calls us to do, with courage, perseverance, and determination. Then, we will see our God-given goals materialize. If we are going to prosper, we have to begin working now on making the right decisions. Those who overcome and endure obstacles are determined to forge ahead and succeed in every endeavor to reach their goals. You will reap the benefits when you choose well. Seasoned warriors position themselves to run the race of victory, despite all the challenges they face. They soar high while accessing the realm which unleashes peak performance, to enlarge their capacity to execute responsibilities from a much higher level. Look at the eagle's existence, they fly high in the sky and are strong. They go to the highest places where their wingspan stretches and widens in any space they chose to fly in. A seasoned warrior does the same thing. They operate and move about with their perception level being eagle-eyed, and are equipped with a far distance sight. They see the real and the unseen in their level of perception, with clarity, and deep depth. **Seasoned warriors are like eagles soaring even higher because they are protected and safe in God's hands.** He wants to give us renewed strength like the eagles. *"Those who hope* *in the Lord will renew their strength. They will soar on wings like eagles; they will run and not grow weary, they will walk and not be faint"* (Isaiah 40:31 NIV).

The enemy has a devious plan to thwart all our endeavors. He wants us to feel unworthy, guilt-ridden, and incompetent when performing our goals. This mindset can damage our self-respect and cause repeated rejections and disappointments as we strive to go forward. This can wear away our confidence and initiative until we lack both the will and desire to forge ahead. This hampers our faith in accomplishing our goals. We must know even though circumstances are always changing; no one is ever alone when encountering such endeavors. We always have the power given to us by our Heavenly Father, His Son Jesus, and the indwelling presence of the Holy Spirit. They are our forever friends and companions, who will never leave or forsake us, and who want us always to succeed. They propel us to go forward as we fulfill the God-inspired goals that lead us to reach our destiny. We all have an assigned destiny that the devil wants us to lose sight of. We must never give in and never give up. We must keep our faith strong because success is for everyone who perseveres through their trials. There is only one loser, and that is the one who throws in the towel because adversity defeats his ambitious quest.

Those who accept the fact that there are obstacles in life, and choose to walk through them with great faith, know how to embrace and endure whatever comes their way. The seasoned warrior is one who is fully conscious of the principle that requires active engagements against adversity. This can only be handled when one's faith in God is fully operative. Wisdom makes known to the warriors their options for victory and the knowledge of how to avoid failure. This is acquired when adversity has tried one's faith, and they know being more in Christ means becoming less in themselves, and making His thoughts greater than theirs. The seasoned warrior stands dressed in the garment of readiness against the devil and all his too familiar lies, snares, and traps. They know his only goal is to rob, steal, and destroy their efforts, and to reduce their effectiveness in following God's path to their destiny. The seasoned warrior remains alert with eyes and ears prepared for readiness. He can count on having other seasoned warriors, sent by God, to help him in battle and to obtain victory. The true warrior operates out of humility, which gives one greater spiritual power. The more we operate in this energetic force, the more successful and happier we become. God will bless and multiply the work and ministry of all those who are meek and humble of heart, both in this life and in the life to come. (Matthew 5:5)

God has given us his Ten Commandments through his servant Moses. He also gave his commandment to his beloved Son, Jesus, to preach the gospel of salvation through grace, and to die for the sins of the whole world. *"And he is the propitiation for our sins: and not for ours only, but also for the sins of the whole world."* 1 John 2:2 (KJV)." Jesus was obedient to His Father's commandments. His ultimate sacrifice of death on the cross was his gift to humanity. Jesus was humble but not weak. He won the battle against Satan by not giving in to his temptations and going willingly to the cross to sacrifice His life for the sins of humanity. By doing this, He defeated the devil's hold over sin and death and gave everyone the right to eternal salvation through him.

God's spiritual powers reside in everyone from birth. We are born in a body that houses our soul and spirit. We are trained by the living Word of God and prepared to fight the good fight for our faith. The Holy Spirit equips us with the knowledge and wisdom of God. The battle against temptation becomes useless if the sinner wants to continue in their sins and succumb to the same temptations and deceptions that Adam and Eve succumbed to when they disobeyed God and ate the forbidden fruit. They were beguiled by Satan's lies that if they ate the fruit from the forbidden tree, they would not die, but become like God knowing good and evil. No good ever comes from disobeying any of God's Ten Commandments, because He does not tolerate disobedience. We must never give in to Satan's temptations. Instead, we need to take up our cross daily and follow our commander in chief, Jesus Christ, into battle with everything that is in us. We must do this daily because Satan is always working and never takes any time off from dispensing his evil darts on humanity.

No one gets through this life without dealing with the unpredictable and uncertainties that creep in everyone's life. Sometimes coping with such trials becomes too challenging to handle on our own. Those who seek God's help should go through the open door to his throne room filled with grace, which is always open. *"Let us then approach God's throne of grace with confidence, so that we may receive mercy and find grace to help us in our time of need"* (Hebrews 4:16 NIV). When God hears the petitions of those in need, He willingly takes over their burden and fights their battles for them. He answers prayers of those who earnestly seek Him, and will see them through their trials with his victory.

No demon can defeat us when we place our faith and trust in God. Those who do become seasoned warriors as they go through the trials and tribulations of life. They become tempered and balanced by the challenges they've overcome because they know it is God who carries them through each and every battle. When life becomes too difficult for us to handle, **God always carries us through our trials and tribulations with triumphs and victory. No one's enemy can defeat God!**

During his earthly life, Jesus had many battles to fight. He triumphed over all of them because He submitted Himself to the will of God. He gave His life so that we may be free from our sins and live eternally in God's kingdom. The Bible clearly states that Jesus overcame every temptation of the devil, and we should as well. Salvation is not a matter of what church you go to or your good deeds; it's a matter of believing in Jesus Christ. He is the true church who gives salvation to all who repent of their sins and accept Him as their Lord and Savior. No amount of good works or any religion can save mankind from their sins. **Jesus is the one and only Savior of mankind.** *"For God so loved the world that he gave his one and only Son, that whoever believes in him shall not perish but have eternal life"* **(John 3:16 NIV).**

Humility is one essential factor that causes warriors to excel in the highest realm. Humility is never a sign of weakness. It shows a great deal of inner strength and character. In Jesus' ministry, He exemplified humility. *"Jesus knew that the Father had put all things under his power, and that he had come from God and was returning to God; so he got up from the meal, took off his outer clothing, and wrapped a towel around his waist. After that, he poured water into a basin and began to wash his disciples' feet, drying them with the towel that was wrapped around him. He came to Simon Peter, who said to him, 'Lord, are you going to wash my feet?' Jesus replied, 'You do not realize now what I am doing, but later you will understand.' 'No,' said Peter, 'you shall never wash my feet.' Jesus answered, 'Unless I wash you, you have no part with me.' 'Then, Lord,' Simon Peter replied, 'not just my feet but my hands and my head as well!' Jesus answered, 'Those who have had a bath need only to wash their feet; their whole body is clean. And you are clean, though not every one of you.' For he knew who was going to betray him, and that was why he said not every one was clean. When he had finished washing their feet, he put on his clothes and returned to his place. 'Do you understand what I have done for you?' he asked them. 'You call me 'Teacher' and 'Lord,' and rightly so, for that is what I am. Now that I, your Lord and Teacher, have washed your feet, you also should wash one another's feet. I have set you an example that you should do as I have done for you. Very truly I tell you, no servant is greater than his master, nor is a messenger greater than the one who sent him. Now that you know these things, you will be blessed if you do them.'"* (John 13:3-17 NIV).

Chapter 26
HOW TO MASTER THE CHANGES IN YOUR LIFE

Mastering the transitions of change in our life requires a willingness to let go of the past along with all our toxic relationships. With faith, God will lead us successfully into the next chapter of our life. Then, we can go forward with the new challenges that lie ahead. Each obstacle we face is a learning and growing experience that clears the way for growth and discovery and connects us to the deeper currents that lead us to our destiny. Life is fashioned by design and is not rooted in an atmosphere of turmoil.

We should nurture others in making their transitions, with wisdom and patience, to help facilitate their movement and momentum in going forward. All the good we do for others is stored up as our treasures in heaven. **No good deed goes unrewarded,** *"The Lord is righteous and loves good deeds; those who do them will live in his presence"* (Psalm 11:7 GNT). *"But store up for yourselves treasures in heaven, where moths and vermin do not destroy, and where thieves do not break in and steal"* (Matthew 6:20 NIV).

Every time transition begins in your life, learn how to master those moments as you walk forward into the light. Then, the revelations of where you are going will be fully illuminated. Pray for discernment to be engraved in your mind and heart. Take each step forward with faith, as you move out of your current status towards your new destination. Mastering this transition involves knowing each stage you are in and the necessary knowledge needed to get to where you're going. If you prayerfully ask God for help, your path will be made straight, *"In all your ways acknowledge Him, And He shall [a]direct your paths"* **(Proverbs 3:6 NKJV).**

Make room for new yearnings and stay connected with those who have learned to consistently increase their faith, while passing from one chapter of their life's journey into the next. Learn to wisely build strategic alliances with those who are both highly resilient and know how to sustain themselves while striving forward to reach their own goals. As iron sharpens iron, and turned-up heat produces fine gold, those placed along the path of uncommon challenges are highly resilient. They know how to sustain and maintain themselves while going forward and reaching their own passionate endeavors. They also make strategic alliances with those who enhance their future goals, so they can arrive at their destination on two feet.

Cleave to the super masters who have learned to increase their wisdom, while passing through new seasons and the stages within them. Expect a shift to emerge, with much from yourself and little from others. Then, along the way, you will avoid incurring resentments, confusion, and disappointments. When everything seems to be going against you, remember that the airplane takes off against the wind, not with it, then lands at its destination. When we travel in the direction of our God-given destiny, we will ultimately land at our destination, through and despite all the underlining currents.

He who controls others may be powerful, but he who has mastered himself has true power. Mastering transition is an inside job that makes room for new and improved yearnings. It usually begins with internal conflict and a feeling of isolation; then, it becomes necessary to evaluate what has taken place externally and how it has affected your decision to go forward. When this happens, it's time to take stock and reassess where you have come from and where you are going in order to have proper alignment with the future that wants to emerge in your life.

Never dwell on the thoughts of those who do not love you. Dwell on thoughts of those who do love you, and those who care about you. Love is God's gift that mends every tear-shed from a broken heart. No person is your friend who demands your silence or denies your right to grow and to be who you were destined to become.

"The most common way people give up their power is by thinking they don't have any." Alice Walker.

A man sees in the world what he carries in his heart. Never be afraid of the greatest enemy of mankind, fear. Be confident in the love and wisdom of God. The path of love may have a thorn along the way, yet love would not be treasured if you did not risk pain to find it. If you do not know who your enemy is, you will be deceived, distracted, and affected by their evil, malicious intent. You must first know who your enemy is. Know how fatal their tongue can be against you and your reputation. Admit they are not trustworthy. Then, **delete them from your life**. This is how you preserve your power and not give it away. Examine your friends and decide on the ones to keep and the ones to walk away from.

True revelation is to recognize that Satan, the devil, is our number one enemy, and all his evil, lustful thoughts and desires must be expelled from our minds. We should not keep fellowship with those who refuse to honor our faith in Jesus Christ. If they can not be converted to Jesus, their destiny is in the ETERNAL

FIRES OF HELL. Don't lull yourself into thinking it is ok to be unevenly yoked with non-believers. When challenges come your way, you have to always be on your guard, especially those with ungodly counsel. Anytime you open up to another and give them your confidence; this increases the potential of their revealing your secrets to others, and having them be distorted. Such trust in man can allow evil forces to come in and cause dissension. This is why we must only trust our innermost private thoughts and desires in God, and not in another person. **We should only seek Godly Counsel for everything.**

> *"Put on the whole armor of God, that you may be able to stand against the wiles of the devil. For we do not wrestle against flesh and blood, but against principalities, against powers, against the rulers of the darkness of this age, against spiritual hosts of wickedness in the heavenly places. Therefore take up the whole armor of God, that you may be able to withstand in the evil day, and having done all, to stand. Stand therefore, having girded your waist with truth, having put on the breastplate of righteousness, and having shod your feet with the preparation of the gospel of peace; above all, taking the shield of faith with which you will be able to quench all the fiery darts of the wicked one. And take the helmet of salvation, and the sword of the Spirit, which is the word of God; praying always with all prayer and supplication in the Spirit, being watchful to this end with all perseverance and supplication for all the saints—and for me, that utterance may be given to me, that I may open my mouth boldly to make known the mystery of the gospel, for which I am an ambassador in chains; that in it I may speak boldly, as I ought to speak"* **(Ephesians 6:11-20 NKJV).**

Love God, keep his commandments, and refrain from doing evil. No one should reason away the quality of life by sinning. This only creates fear, which determines the road we travel on. Keep yourself healthy and happy by living without fear. Be free like a bird that flies with a purpose. Even though birds take time out to rest and commune with nature, they can soar to infinite heights. When we avoid sin, we, too, can be free like the birds and soar through life with a free conscience and enjoy life to its fullest. Contentment with peace of mind is the reward for a life free from sin. Everyone faces temptations from Satan. We must do what Jesus did when Satan tempted Him in the wilderness, after He fasted for 40 days and 40 nights, and was weakened by the lack of nourishment. He rejected Satan's three temptations with the Word of God. God will not allow us to be overtaken by temptation. *"No temptation has overtaken you except what is common to mankind. And God is faithful; he will not let you be tempted beyond what you can bear. But when you are tempted, he will also provide a way out so that you can endure it"* (Deuteronomy 5:22-27 NIV).

Life can be your most cherished spiritual teacher. An observant adventurer has outgrown and disowned negative thoughts that can limit, hinder, or devalue their ability to reach their goals. Detoxifying the deadening effects of faulty beliefs will clear your mind to seek new doors of opportunity and explore new horizons. This world offers countless blessings to a happy adventurer who is well aware of the inner strength that propels him to use his capabilities to move forward and avoids the strongholds that bind him. Spends quality time in quiet solitude and reflects on every phase of your journey. Seeks to learn all that is necessary from life's experience. With an open mind, you can think and reflect on advice from the best life-long learners who continually experience an increase in wisdom. Don't let anyone make you feel like you don't deserve what you want. Above all, be true to yourself. If you cannot put your heart into something, take yourself out of it. When the road gets rough, you need to figure out who stands behind you and who does not. You will not move into the supernatural until you have embraced the natural with faith and courage.

King David learned so much by spending time alone in the solitude of the wilderness while keeping watch over his sheep. The greater the time spent alone, the greater the learning, and the greater preparation for leadership. As a young teenager, David started out as a sheepherder to being called by God to lead the nation of Israel as their second king. God had Prophet Samuel inform David, when he was between 10 and 15 years old, that he would step out of his role as a shepherd to being the King of Israel and replace King Saul after his death. David was 30 years old when Samuel anointed him king, and he ruled Israel for 40 years. The best place to mold one's spirit is to be in communion with God. During this time, David wrote 70 psalms in the Book of Psalms, which are incredibly enriching to one's soul. When we meditate on God's Word, He is pleased. He wants us to get understanding and to exalt wisdom. ***"The beginning of wisdom is this: Get wisdom. Though it cost all you have, get understanding. Cherish her, and she will exalt you; embrace her, and she will honor you"*** **(Proverbs 4:7-8 NIV).** Wisdom is the first and highest gift from the Holy Spirit to value the things we believe through faith. Wisdom leads to an intimate understanding of God's word, his Ten Commandments, and having a holy and righteous life.

God's words are powerful and can not come back to him void. What he says he will do, he does. There is only one thing God can not do, and that is lie. *"God is not a man, that He should lie, Nor a son of man, that He should repent. Has He said, and will He not do? Or has He spoken, and will He not make it good?"* (Numbers 23:19 NKJV). The safest place for our heart and soul is to be in the hands of God and not man or ourselves. God gave mankind His best, His only begotten Son Jesus. He wants us to honor Him with love, trust, and servant-ship. He is good, faithful, and true. Everyone was created for Him and by Him.

Jesus freely went to the cross to die as atonement for all our sins. Through His sacrifice, we are offered unmerited favor, forgiveness for all our sins, and eternal salvation. All we have to do is repent of our sins and make Jesus the Lord of our life. Those who reject God's free gift of grace will pay the penalty for their own sins by spending an eternity in the fires of hell. God wants everyone to choose life and not death. *"I call heaven and earth as witnesses today against you, that I have set before you life and death, blessing and cursing; therefore choose life, that both you and your descendants may live"* **(Deuteronomy 30:19 NKJV).**

We all have decisions to make in this life, some serious and some not so serious. Nevertheless, the right decisions enhance our life, and the wrong decisions can be a turning point to disaster. There will be people we need to deal with, and those we don't want to deal with. We need to choose wisely those who are to stay in our lives and those we walk away from. Trustworthiness is a necessary quality when we choose who to bring into our lives and who to keep out. We should use discernment and only choose those who trust in God because they are moved by faith in divine revelation and not in their own personal self. There is only one way to receive the supernatural gift of discernment, and that's through God's Holy Spirit.

Chapter 27

THE TEN COMMANDMENTS AND THE BOOK OF THE LAW

God gave Moses the Ten Commandments written by His own finger on two tablets of stone. Moses told the Israelites of his vision from God and the details of his receiving the Ten Commandments, *"These words the Lord spoke to all your assembly, in the mountain from the midst of the fire, the cloud, and the thick darkness, with a loud voice; and He added no more. And He wrote them on two tablets of stone and gave them to me. So it was, when you heard the voice from the midst of the darkness, while the mountain was burning with fire, that you came near to me, all the heads of your tribes and your elders. And you said: 'Surely the Lord our God has shown us His glory and His greatness, and we have heard His voice from the midst of the fire. We have seen this day that God speaks with man; yet he still lives. Now therefore, why should we die? For this great fire will consume us; if we hear the voice of the Lord our God anymore, then we shall die. For who is there of all flesh who has heard the voice of the living God speaking from the midst of the fire, as we have, and lived? You go near and hear all that the Lord our God may say, and tell us all that the Lord our God says to you, and we will hear and do it'"* (Deuteronomy 5:22-27 NKJV).

To house the Ten Commandments, God gave instructions for Moses to build the Ark of the Covenant.

149

"And they shall make an ark of acacia wood; two and a half cubits shall be its length, a cubit and a half its width, and a cubit and a half its height. 11 And you shall overlay it with pure gold, inside and out you shall overlay it, and shall make on it a molding of gold all around. You shall cast four rings of gold for it, and put them in its four corners; two rings shall be on one side, and two rings on the other side. And you shall make poles of acacia wood, and overlay them with gold. You shall put the poles into the rings on the sides of the ark, that the ark may be carried by them. The poles shall be in the rings of the ark; they shall not be taken from it. And you shall put into the ark the Testimony which I will give you.

You shall make a mercy seat of pure gold; two and a half cubits shall be its length and a cubit and a half its width. And you shall make two cherubim of gold; of hammered work you shall make them at the two ends of the mercy seat. Make one cherub at one end, and the other cherub at the other end; you shall make the cherubim at the two ends of it of one piece with the mercy seat. And the cherubim shall stretch out their wings above, covering the mercy seat with their wings, and they shall face one another; the faces of the cherubim shall be toward the mercy seat. You shall put the mercy seat on top of the ark, and in the ark you shall put the Testimony that I will give you. And there I will meet with you, and I will speak with you from above the mercy seat, from between the two cherubim which are on the ark of the Testimony, about everything which I will give you in commandment to the children of Israel" (Exodus 25:10-22 NKJV).

The Mosaic Law, according to the Old Testament, was given by God to the Israelites through Moses and included the many rules of religious observance recorded in the first five books of the Old Testament. In Judaism, these books are called the Torah, or "the law."

The Book of the Law was put in the side of the Ark of the Covenant as a witness against the Israelites. *"Take this Book of the Law, and put it beside the ark of the covenant of the Lord your God, that it may be there as a witness against you"* (Deuteronomy 31:26 NKJV).

The Ten Commandments can be found in both the Old and New Testaments

OLD TESTAMENT

I. *"Thou shalt have no other gods before me"* (Exodus 20:3 KJV).

II. *"Thou shalt not make unto thee any graven image, or any likeness of anything that is in heaven above, or that is in the earth beneath, or that is in the water under the earth"* (Exodus 20:4 KJV).

III. *"Thou shalt not take the name of the lord thy god in vain; for the Lord will not hold him guiltless that taketh his name in vain"* Exodus 20:7 KJV).

IV. *"Remember the sabbath day, to keep it holy"* (Exodus 20:8 KJV).

V. *"Honor thy father and thy mother: that thy days may be long upon the land which the lord thy god giveth thee"* (Exodus 20:9 KJV).

VI. *"Thou shalt not kill"* (Exodus 20:13 KJV).

VII. *"Thou shalt not commit adultery"* (Exodus 20:14 KJV).

VIII. *"Thou shalt not steal"* (Exodus 20:15 KJV).

IX. *"Thou shalt not bear false witness against thy neighbor"* (Exodus 20:16 KJV).

X. *"Thou shalt not covet thy neighbor's house, thou shalt not covet thy neighbor's wife, nor his manservant, nor his maidservant, nor his ox, nor his ass, nor any thing that is thy neighbor's"* (Exodus 20:17 KJV).

NEW TESTAMENT

I. *"Jesus said unto him, **Thou shalt love the Lord thy God with all thy heart,** and with all thy soul, and with all thy mind. This is the first and great commandment"* (Matthew 22:37-38 KJV).

II. *"**God is a Spirit**: and they that worship Him **must worship him in spirit** and in truth"* (John 4:24 KJV).

III. *"**For out of the heart proceed** evil thoughts, murders, adulteries, fornications, thefts, false witness, [and] **blasphemies**"* (Matthew 15:19 KJV).

IV. *"He came to Nazareth, where He had been brought up: and, as His custom was, **He went into the synagogue on the sabbath day**, and stood up for to read"* (Luke 4:16 KJV).

V. *"**Honour thy father and thy mother**: and, Thou shalt love thy neighbour as thyself"* (Matthew 19:19 KJV).

VI. *"Jesus said, **Thou shalt do no murder**, Thou shalt not commit adultery, Thou shalt not steal, Thou shalt not bear false witness"* (Matthew 19:18 KJV).

VII. *"What shall we say then? Is the law sin? God forbid. Nay, I had not known sin, but by the law: for I had not known lust, except the law had said, **Thou shalt not covet**"* (Romans 7:7 KJV).

Knowing God's Laws are forever, Jesus never said He came to destroy God's Ten Commandments. Instead, He said He came to fulfill the law and the prophets as quoted in the following scriptures:

Matthew 5:17 KJV

"Think not that i am come to destroy the law, or the prophets: i am not come to destroy, but to fulfil."

Luke 16:17 KJV

"It is easier for heaven and earth to pass, than one tittle of the law to fail."

Rom. 7:7 KJV

"What shall we say then? Is the law sin? God forbid. Nay, I had not known sin, but by the law: for I had not known lust, except the law had said, Thou shalt not covet."

Rom. 3:20 KJV

"Therefore by the deeds of the law there shall no flesh be justified in his sight: for by the law is the knowledge of sin."

Col. 2:14 KJV

"Blotting out the handwriting of ordinances that was against us, which was contrary to us, and took it out of the way, nailing it to his cross."

1 John 5:3 KJV

"For this is the love of God, that we keep his commandments: and his commandments are not grievous."

When Jesus was asked by the Pharisees, to identify the greatest commandments, He responded, *"Love the Lord your God with all your heart and with all your soul and with all your mind. This is the first and greatest commandment. And the second is like it: Love your neighbor as yourself"* (Matthew 22:37-39 NIV).

Sinners are saved by faith in God's grace and through Jesus Christ. **Those who trust in Jesus are not under the law; they are saved under grace**. Apostle Paul says, *"Sin shall no longer be your master, because you are not under the law, but under grace"* (Romans 6:14 NIV). This does not mean that people are now free to sin. It is the law that continually reminds sinners of their need for Christ and their inability to attain salvation in their own strength. When the law has served this function, a sinner is driven to God's grace in Jesus. The law is a reflection of God's character and an expression of who He is. Just as the law corresponds to God's nature, those made in His image also correspond to his nature. **God gave his Ten Commandments because He loves us. Satan wants everyone to break God's Laws because he hates God and us.**

Chapter 28
GOD BLESSED THE SEVENTH DAY
AS A SABBATH REST FOR MAN

After creating the universe and everything in it in six days, *"God blessed the seventh day and sanctified it, because in it He rested from all His work which God had created and made"* (Genesis 2:3 NKJV). He made the seventh day a sabbath as his Fourth Commandment, and said, *"Remember the sabbath day, to keep it holy. Six days shalt thou labour, and do all thy work: But the seventh day is the sabbath of the Lord thy God: in it thou shalt not do any work, thou, nor thy son, nor thy daughter, thy manservant, nor thy maidservant, nor thy cattle, nor thy stranger that is within thy gates: For in six days the Lord made heaven and earth, the sea, and all that in them is, and rested the seventh day: wherefore the Lord blessed the sabbath day, and hallowed it"* (Exodus 20:8-11 NKJV).

Our bodies, like a flashlight, can shine a great distance on a full charge. Periodically, we need to recharge our bodies. Obeying God's Fourth Commandment, as a day of rest, allows not only our body to be refreshed and rejuvenated, but our mind and spirit as well. This is a day God set aside for us to commune with Him, as well as rest from our labors. The seventh day is symbolic of God completing creation in six days and resting from all His works on the seventh day, even though he does not get tired as we do. The seventh day is the only day of the week he blessed and set aside as an example of what we must also do. *"Then God blessed the seventh day and made it holy, because on it He rested from all the work of creating that He had done"* (Genesis 2:3 NIV).

Satan wants to obscure the value and the health benefits from taking this day as a day of rest. Jesus confirmed keeping the weekly sabbath, and he also kept the annual sabbaths as well. Jesus said, *"The Sabbath was made for man, not man for the Sabbath"* (Mark 2:27 NIV).

GOD'S FOURTH COMMANDMENT IS REPEATED THROUGHOUT THE BIBLE

Genesis 2:2-3 NIV

"By the seventh day God had finished the work he had been doing; so, on the seventh day he rested from all his work. Then God blessed the seventh day and made it Holy, because on it He rested from all the work of creating that He had done.

Exodus 20:8-11 NIV

"Remember the Sabbath day by keeping it Holy. Six days you shall labor and do all your work, but the seventh day is a sabbath to the Lord your God. On it you shall not do any work, neither you, nor your son or daughter, nor your male or female servant, nor your animals, nor any foreigner residing in your towns. For in six days the Lord made the heavens and the earth, the sea, and all that is in them, but He rested on the seventh day. Therefore the Lord blessed the Sabbath day and made it Holy."

Deuteronomy 5:13-14 NIV

"Six days you shall labor and do all your work, but the seventh day is a sabbath to the Lord your God. On it you shall not do any

work, neither you, nor your son or daughter, nor your male or female servant, nor your ox, your donkey or any of your animals, nor any foreigner residing in your towns, so that your male and female servants may rest, as you do."

Exodus 20:8 NIV

"Remember the Sabbath day by keeping it Holy."

Exodus 31:14 NIV

"Observe the Sabbath, because it is holy to you. Anyone who desecrates it is to be put to death; those who do any work on that day must be cut off from their people."

Hebrews 4:9 NIV

"There remains, then, a Sabbath-rest for the people of God"

Leviticus 23:3 NIV

"There are six days when you may work, but the seventh day is a day of sabbath rest, a day of sacred assembly. You are not to do any work; wherever you live, it is a sabbath to the Lord."

Mark 2:27 NIV

"Then he said to them, 'The Sabbath was made for man, not man for the Sabbath.'"

Matthew 24:20 NIV

"Pray that your flight will not take place in winter or on the Sabbath."

Chapter 29
GOD CREATED ALL THINGS THROUGH JESUS

Six thousand years ago, God created matter, for Jesus to frame and create the heavens and the earth. *"By faith we understand that the worlds were framed by the word of God, so that the things which are seen were not made of things which are visible"* (Hebrews 11:3 NKJV). God created man from the dust of the earth. *"Then the Lord God formed a man from the dust of the ground and breathed into his nostrils the breath of life, and the man became a living being"* (Hebrews 11:3 NIV).

Creation of the universe came into existence by God's Word, His will, and His almighty power. He created all things through his only begotten Son, Jesus. Everything was made for Him and by Him, and nothing was made without Him. ***"For by Him all things were created that are in heaven and that are on earth, visible and invisible, whether thrones or dominions or principalities or powers. All things were created through Him and for Him"*** **(Colossians 1:16 NKJV).**

Jesus not only created man but willingly gave up His life on the cross as atonement for their sins. He was resurrected back to life after being sealed in a stone tomb for three days and three nights. His death on the cross, resurrection, and his visual ascension to heaven was witnessed by over five hundred people. *"For what I received I passed on to you as of first importance: that Christ died for our sins according to the Scriptures, that he was buried, that he was raised on the third day according to the Scriptures, and that he appeared to Cephas,and then to the Twelve. After that, he appeared to more than five hundred of the brothers and sisters at the same time, most of whom are still living, though some have fallen asleep. Then he appeared to James, then to all the apostles, and last of all he appeared to me also, as to one abnormally born"* (1 Corinthians 15:3-8 NIV).

During Jesus' entire life, he exhibited his deity. With such worldwide evidence, no logically thinking person can deny the fact that Jesus is the son of God and the Savior of mankind. The Word of God confirms this truth. The Bible attests to his deity. Historical documented facts and witnesses confirm the evidence of Jesus' life, death, resurrection, and ascension to heaven. It is only through Jesus that we have forgiveness for our sins and the promise of eternal life in heaven. The oldest book in the world, the Bible, and the prophets in the old and new testaments declare that Jesus is the Son of God. Only Jesus could perform such miracles as bringing the dead back to life, and countless other signs and wonders that can only be performed by God's Son, our creator. Those whose hearts do not dwell by faith in Christ will be consumed by the world, Satan, and the fires of hell.

Since his ascension, Jesus stands at the right hand of the Father. Before the final Battle of Armageddon, He will return to rapture those who believe in Him and bring them to their eternal home in heaven. Two thousand years ago, Apostle Stephen had a vision of Jesus while he was being stoned by the same crowd who had crucified Jesus. Before Stephen took his last breath, he gazed up into heaven and saw the glory of God and Jesus standing at his right hand. *"But Stephen, full of the Holy Spirit, looked up to heaven and saw the glory of God, and Jesus standing at the right hand of God. 'Look,' he said, 'I see heaven open and the Son of Man standing at the right hand of God'"* (Acts 7:55-56 NIV). Everyone needs to keep this vision alive in their minds because Jesus is alive and at the right hand of God as our Savior, Intercessor, and Mediator.

Soon, He will rapture all His saints who believe in Him and bring us to our eternal home in heaven! In the meantime, Jesus is at the right hand of God interceding for us, while Satan is the accuser of the brethren.

"Who is he that condemneth? It is Christ that died, yea rather, that is risen again, who is even at the right hand of God, who also maketh intercession for us" (**Romans 8:34 KJV**).

"And I heard a loud voice saying in heaven, Now is come salvation, and strength, and the kingdom of our God, and the power of his Christ: for the accuser of our brethren is cast down, which accused them before our God day and night" (Revelation 12:1 KJV.)

Chapter 30
JESUS' SUPERNATURAL MIRACLES

Jesus' first supernatural event was His **virgin birth**. He was conceived by the Holy Spirit in the womb of a young virgin named Mary. This supernatural event was prophesized in the Garden of Eden after the fall of Adam and Eve, *"Her offspring will crush your head"* (Genesis 3:15 GNT). The prophecy of Jesus' virginal conception and being named Immanuel, which means "God with us," was confirmed in the Book of Isaiah, ***"Therefore the Lord Himself will give you a sign: Behold, the virgin shall conceive and bear a Son, and shall call His name Immanuel" (Isaiah 7:14 NKJV).***

The Gospels record numerous supernatural miracles that Jesus performed during his earthly ministry. Many of these miracles are detailed below. Apostle John further records, *"Jesus did many other things as well. If every one of them were written down, I suppose that even the whole world would not have room for the books that would be written"* (John 21:25 NIV). Jesus declared, *"But I have a greater witness than John's; for the works which the Father has given Me to finish—the very works that I do—bear witness of Me, that the Father has sent Me"* (John 5:36 NKJV).

Jesus' first miracle at the beginning of His three-and-a-half-year ministry was to honor His mother's request to change water into wine at the wedding in Cana.

"On the third day a wedding took place at Cana in Galilee. Jesus' mother was there, and Jesus and his disciples had also been invited to the wedding. When the wine was gone, Jesus' mother said to him, 'They have no more wine.'

'Woman, why do you involve me?' Jesus replied. 'My hour has not yet come.'

His mother said to the servants, 'Do whatever he tells you.'

Nearby stood six stone water jars, the kind used by the Jews for ceremonial washing, each holding from twenty to thirty gallons. Jesus said to the servants, 'Fill the jars with water'; so they filled them to the brim.

Then he told them, 'Now draw some out and take it to the master of the banquet.'

They did so, and the master of the banquet tasted the water that had been turned into wine. He did not realize where it had come from, though the servants who had drawn the water knew. Then he called the bridegroom aside and said, 'Everyone brings out the choice wine first and then the cheaper wine after the guests have had too much to drink; but you have saved the best till now.'

What Jesus did here in Cana of Galilee was the first of the signs through which he revealed his glory; and his disciples believed in him" (John 2:1-11 NIV)

THESE SUPERNATURAL MIRACLES OF HEALING WERE PERFORMED BY JESUS:

Healing of the Royal Official's Son

"Once more he visited Cana in Galilee, where he had turned the water into wine. And there was a certain royal official whose son

lay sick at Capernaum. When this man heard that Jesus had arrived in Galilee from Judea, he went to him and begged him to come and heal his son, who was close to death. 'Unless you people see signs and wonders,' Jesus told him, 'you will never believe.' The royal official said, "'Sir, come down before my child dies.' 'Go,' Jesus replied, 'your son will live.' The man took Jesus at his word and departed. While he was still on the way, his servants met him with the news that his boy was living. When he inquired as to the time when his son got better, they said to him, 'Yesterday, at one in the afternoon, the fever left him.' Then the father realized that this was the exact time at which Jesus had said to him, 'Your son will live.' So he and his whole household believed. This was the second sign Jesus performed after coming from Judea to Galilee" (John 4:46-54 NIV).

Healing of a Man Possessed by a Demon

"In the synagogue there was a man possessed by a demon, an impure spirit. He cried out at the top of his voice, 'Go away! What do you want with us, Jesus of Nazareth? Have you come to destroy us? I know who you are—the Holy One of God!' 'Be quiet!' Jesus said sternly. 'Come out of him!' Then the demon threw the man down before them all and came out without injuring him. All the people were amazed and said to each other, 'What words these are! With authority and power he gives orders to impure spirits and they come out!' And the news about him spread throughout the surrounding area" (Luke 4:33-37 NIV).

Healing of Simon Peter's Mother-in-Law

"When Jesus came into Peter's house, he saw Peter's mother-in-law lying in bed with a fever. He touched her hand and the fever left her, and she got up and began to wait on him" (Matthew 8:14-15 NIV).

Healing the Sick During the Evening

"At sunset, the people brought to Jesus all who had various kinds of sickness, and laying his hands on each one, he healed them" (Luke 4:40 NIV).

Healing a Leper

"When Jesus came down from the mountainside, large crowds followed him. A man with leprosy came and knelt before him and said, 'Lord, if you are willing, you can make me clean.' Jesus reached out his hand and touched the man. 'I am willing,' he said. 'Be clean!' Immediately he was cleansed of his leprosy" (Matthew 8:1-4 NIV).

Healing a Centurion's Servant

"When Jesus had finished saying all this to the people who were listening, he entered Capernaum. There a centurion's servant, whom his master valued highly, was sick and about to die. The centurion heard of Jesus and sent some elders of the Jews to him, asking him to come and heal his servant. When they came to Jesus, they pleaded earnestly with him, 'This man deserves to have you do this, because he loves our nation and has built our synagogue.' So Jesus went with them. He was not far from the house when the centurion sent friends to say to him: 'Lord, don't trouble yourself, for I do not deserve to have you come under my roof. That is why I did not even consider myself worthy to come to you. But say the word, and my servant will be healed. For I myself am a man under authority, with soldiers under me. I tell this one, 'Go,' and he goes; and that one, 'Come,' and he comes. I say to my servant, 'Do this,' and he does it.' When Jesus heard this, he was amazed at him, and turning to the crowd following him, he said, 'I tell you, I have not found such great faith even in Israel.' Then the men who had been sent returned to the house and found the servant well" (Luke 7:1-10 NIV).

Healing a Paralyzed Man

"Jesus stepped into a boat, crossed over and came to his own town. Some men brought to him a paralyzed man, lying on a mat. When Jesus saw their faith, he said to the man, 'Take heart, son; your sins are forgiven.' At this, some of the teachers of the law said to themselves, 'This fellow is blaspheming!' Knowing their thoughts, Jesus said, 'Why do you entertain evil thoughts in your hearts? Which is easier: to say, 'Your sins are forgiven,' or to say, 'Get up and walk'? 'But I want you to know that the Son of Man has authority on earth to forgive sins.' So he said to the paralyzed man, 'Get up, take your mat and go home.' Then the man got up and went home. When the crowd saw this, they were filled with awe; and they praised God, who had given such authority to man" (Luke 7:1-10 NIV).

Healing a Withered Hand

"Another time Jesus went into the synagogue, and a man with a shriveled hand was there. Some of them were looking for a reason to accuse Jesus, so they watched him closely to see if he would heal him on the Sabbath. Jesus said to the man with the shriveled hand, 'Stand up in front of everyone.' Then Jesus asked them, 'Which is lawful on the Sabbath: to do good or to do evil, to save life or to kill?' But they remained silent. He looked around at them in anger and, deeply distressed at their stubborn hearts, said to the man, 'Stretch out your hand.' He stretched it out, and his hand was completely restored" (Mark 3:1-5 NIV).

Raising a Widow's Son

"Soon afterward, Jesus went to a town called Nain, and his disciples and a large crowd went along with him. As he approached the town gate, a dead person was being carried out—the only son of his mother, and she was a widow. And a large crowd from the

town was with her. When the Lord saw her, his heart went out to her and he said, 'Don't cry.' Then he went up and touched the bier they were carrying him on, and the bearers stood still. He said, 'Young man, I say to you, get up!' The dead man sat up and began to talk, and Jesus gave him back to his mother. They were all filled with awe and praised God. 'A great prophet has appeared among us,' they said. 'God has come to help his people.' This news about Jesus spread throughout Judea and the surrounding country" (Luke 7:11-17 NIV).

Healing the Gerasene Demon-Possessed Man

"When he arrived at the other side in the region of the Gadarenes, two demon-possessed men coming from the tombs met him. They were so violent that no one could pass that way. 'What do you want with us, Son of God?' they shouted. 'Have you come here to torture us before the appointed time?' Some distance from them a large herd of pigs was feeding. The demons begged Jesus, 'If you drive us out, send us into the herd of pigs.' He said to them, 'Go!' So they came out and went into the pigs, and the whole herd rushed down the steep bank into the lake and died in the water" (Matthew 8:28-32 NIV).

Healing a Woman with Internal Bleeding

"And a woman was there who had been subject to bleeding for twelve years. She had suffered a great deal under the care of many doctors and had spent all she had, yet instead of getting better she grew worse. When she heard about Jesus, she came up behind him in the crowd and touched his cloak, because she thought, 'If I just touch his clothes, I will be healed.' Immediately her bleeding stopped, and she felt in her body that she was freed from her suffering. At once Jesus realized that power had gone out from him. He turned around in the crowd and asked, 'Who touched my clothes?' 'You see the people crowding against you,' his disciples *answered, 'and yet you can ask, 'Who touched me?'' But Jesus kept looking around to see who had done it. Then the woman, knowing what had happened to her, came and fell at his feet and, trembling with fear, told him the whole truth. He said to her, 'Daughter, your faith has healed you. Go in peace and be freed from your suffering'"* (Mark 5:25-34 NIV).

Raising Jairus' Daughter

"While Jesus was still speaking, someone came from the house of Jairus, the synagogue leader. 'Your daughter is dead,' he said. 'Don't bother the teacher anymore.' Hearing this, Jesus said to Jairus, 'Don't be afraid; just believe, and she will be healed.' When he arrived at the house of Jairus, he did not let anyone go in with him except Peter, John and James, and the child's father and mother. Meanwhile, all the people were wailing and mourning for her. 'Stop wailing,' Jesus said. 'She is not dead but asleep.' They laughed at him, knowing that she was dead. But he took her by the hand and said, 'My child, get up!' Her spirit returned, and at once she stood up. Then Jesus told them to give her something to eat. Her parents were astonished, but he ordered them not to tell anyone what had happened" (Luke 8:49-56 NIV).

Healing Two Blind Men

"As Jesus went on from there, two blind men followed him, calling out, 'Have mercy on us, Son of David!' When he had gone indoors, the blind men came to him, and he asked them, 'Do you believe that I am able to do this?' 'Yes, Lord,' they replied. Then he touched their eyes and said, 'According to your faith let it be done to you'; and their sight was restored. Jesus warned them sternly, 'See that no one knows about this.' But they went out and spread the news about him all over that region" (Matthew 9:27-31 NIV).

Healing a Mute Man Possessed by a Demon

"While they were going out, a man who was demon-possessed and could not talk was brought to Jesus. And when the demon was driven out, the man who had been mute spoke. The crowd was amazed and said, 'Nothing like this has ever been seen in Israel'" (Matthew 9:32-33 NIV).

Healing a Man Who Was Crippled for Thirty-Eight Years

"Some time later, Jesus went up to Jerusalem for one of the Jewish festivals. Now there is in Jerusalem near the Sheep Gate a pool, which in Aramaic is called Bethesda and which is surrounded by five covered colonnades. Here a great number of disabled people used to lie—the blind, the lame, the paralyzed. One who was there had been an invalid for thirty-eight years. When Jesus saw him lying there and learned that he had been in this condition for a long time, he asked him, 'Do you want to get well?' 'Sir,' the invalid replied, 'I have no one to help me into the pool when the water is stirred. While I am trying to get in, someone else goes down ahead of me.' Then Jesus said to him, 'Get up! Pick up your mat and walk.' At once the man was cured; he picked up his mat and walked" (John 5:1-9 NIV).

Healing of Many in Gennesaret

"When they had crossed over, they landed at Gennesaret and anchored there. As soon as they got out of the boat, people recognized Jesus. They ran throughout that whole region and carried the sick on mats to wherever they heard he was. And wherever he went—into villages, towns or countryside—they placed the sick in the marketplaces. They begged him to let them touch even the edge of his cloak, and all who touched it were healed" (Mark 6:53-56 NIV).

Healing a Demon-Possessed Girl

"Leaving that place, Jesus withdrew to the region of Tyre and Sidon. A Canaanite woman from that vicinity came to him, crying out, 'Lord, Son of David, have mercy on me! My daughter is demon-possessed and suffering terribly.' Jesus did not answer a word. So his disciples came to him and urged him, 'Send her away, for she keeps crying out after us.' He answered, 'I was sent only to the lost sheep of Israel.' The woman came and knelt before him. 'Lord, help me!' she said. He replied, 'It is not right to take the children's bread and toss it to the dogs.' 'Yes it is, Lord,' she said. 'Even the dogs eat the crumbs that fall from their master's table.' Then Jesus said to her, 'Woman, you have great faith! Your request is granted.' And her daughter was healed at that moment" (Matthew 15:21-28 NIV).

Healing a Deaf Man With a Speech Impediment

"Then Jesus left the vicinity of Tyre and went through Sidon, down to the Sea of Galilee and into the region of the Decapolis. There some people brought to him a man who was deaf and could hardly talk, and they begged Jesus to place his hand on him. After he took him aside, away from the crowd, Jesus put his fingers into the man's ears. Then he spit and touched the man's tongue. He looked up to heaven and with a deep sigh said to him, 'Ephphatha!' (which means 'Be opened!'). At this, the man's ears were opened, his tongue was loosened and he began to speak plainly. Jesus commanded them not to tell anyone. But the more he did so, the more they kept talking about it. People were overwhelmed with amazement. 'He has done everything well,' they said. 'He even makes the deaf hear and the mute speak'" (Mark 7:31-37 NIV).

Feeding Four Thousand Men and Their Families

"Jesus left there and went along the Sea of Galilee. Then he went up on a mountainside and sat down. Great crowds came to him, bringing the lame, the blind, the crippled, the mute and many others, and laid them at his feet; and he healed them. The people were amazed when they saw the mute speaking, the crippled made well, the lame walking and the blind seeing. And they praised the God of Israel. Jesus called his disciples to him and said, 'I have compassion for these people; they have already been with me three days and have nothing to eat. I do not want to send them away hungry, or they may collapse on the way.' His disciples answered, 'Where could we get enough bread in this remote place to feed such a crowd?' 'How many loaves do you have?' Jesus asked. 'Seven,' they replied, 'and a few small fish.' He told the crowd to sit down on the ground. Then he took the seven loaves and the fish, and when he had given thanks, he broke them and gave them to the disciples, and they in turn to the people. They all ate and were satisfied. Afterward the disciples picked up seven basketfuls of broken pieces that were left over. The number of those who ate was four thousand men, besides women and children" (Mark 7:31-37 NIV).

Healing a Blind Man in Bethsaida

"They came to Bethsaida, and some people brought a blind man and begged Jesus to touch him. He took the blind man by the hand and led him outside the village. When he had spit on the man's eyes and put his hands on him, Jesus asked, 'Do you see anything?' He looked up and said, 'I see people; they look like trees walking around.' Once more Jesus put his hands on the man's eyes. Then his eyes were opened, his sight was restored, and he saw everything clearly. Jesus sent him home, saying, 'Don't even go into the village'" (mark 8:22-26 NIV).

Healing a Man Born Blind

"As he went along, he saw a man blind from birth. His disciples asked him, 'Rabbi, who sinned, this man or his parents, that he was born blind?' 'Neither this man nor his parents sinned,' said Jesus, 'but this happened so that the works of God might be displayed in him. As long as it is day, we must do the works of him who sent me. Night is coming, when no one can work. While I am in the world, I am the light of the world.' After saying this, he spit on the ground, made some mud with the saliva, and put it on the man's eyes. 'Go,' he told him, 'wash in the Pool of Siloam.' So the man went and washed, and came home seeing. His neighbors and those who had formerly seen him begging asked, 'Isn't this the same man who used to sit and beg?' Some claimed that he was. Others said, 'No, he only looks like him.' But he himself insisted, 'I am the man.' 'How then were your eyes opened?' they asked. He replied, 'The man they call Jesus made some mud and put it on my eyes. He told me to go to Siloam and wash. So I went and washed, and then I could see'" (John 9: 1-11 NIV).

Healing a Boy Possessed by a Demon

"When they came to the crowd, a man approached Jesus and knelt before him. 'Lord, have mercy on my son,' he said. 'He has seizures and is suffering greatly. He often falls into the fire or into the water. I brought him to your disciples, but they could not heal him.' 'You unbelieving and perverse generation,' Jesus replied, 'how long shall I stay with you? How long shall I put up with you? Bring the boy here to me.' Jesus rebuked the demon, and it came out of the boy, and he was healed at that moment" (Matthew 17:14-18 NIV).

Healing a Blind and Mute Man Who Was Possessed by a Demon

"Jesus was driving out a demon that was mute. When the demon left, the man who had been mute spoke, and the crowd was amazed" (Luke 11:14 NIV).

Healing a Woman With an Eighteen-Year Infirmity

"On a Sabbath Jesus was teaching in one of the synagogues, and a woman was there who had been crippled by a spirit for eighteen years. She was bent over and could not straighten up at all. When Jesus saw her, he called her forward and said to her, 'Woman, you are set free from your infirmity.' Then he put his hands on her, and immediately she straightened up and praised God" (Luke 13:10-13 NIV).

Healing a Man With Dropsy

"One Sabbath, when Jesus went to eat in the house of a prominent Pharisee, he was being carefully watched. There in front of him was a man suffering from abnormal swelling of his body. Jesus asked the Pharisees and experts in the law, 'Is it lawful to heal on the Sabbath or not?' But they remained silent. So taking hold of the man, he healed him and sent him on his way. Then he asked them, 'If one of you has a child or an ox that falls into a well on the Sabbath day, will you not immediately pull it out?' And they had nothing to say" (Luke 14:1-6 NIV).

Healing Ten Men Suffering From Leprosy

"Now on his way to Jerusalem, Jesus traveled along the border between Samaria and Galilee. As he was going into a village, ten men who had leprosy met him. They stood at a distance and called out in a loud voice, 'Jesus, Master, have pity on us!' When he saw them, he said, 'Go, show yourselves to the priests.' And as they

went, they were cleansed. One of them, when he saw he was healed, came back, praising God in a loud voice. He threw himself at Jesus' feet and thanked him—and he was a Samaritan. Jesus asked, 'Were not all ten cleansed? Where are the other nine? Has no one returned to give praise to God except this foreigner?' Then he said to him, 'Rise and go; your faith has made you well.'" (Luke 17:11-19 NIV).

Bringing Lazarus Back to Life

"1 Now a man named Lazarus was sick. He was from Bethany, the village of Mary and her sister Martha.

2 (This Mary, whose brother Lazarus now lay sick, was the same one who poured perfume on the Lord and wiped his feet with her hair.)

3 So the sisters sent word to Jesus, "Lord, the one you love is sick."

4 When he heard this, Jesus said, "This sickness will not end in death. No, it is for God's glory so that God's Son may be glorified through it."

5 Now Jesus loved Martha and her sister and Lazarus.

6 So when he heard that Lazarus was sick, he stayed where he was two more days,

7 and then he said to his disciples, "Let us go back to Judea."

8 "But Rabbi," they said, "a short while ago the Jews there tried to stone you, and yet you are going back?"

9 Jesus answered, "Are there not twelve hours of daylight? Anyone who walks in the daytime will not stumble, for they see by this world's light.

10 It is when a person walks at night that they stumble, for they have no light."

11 *After he had said this, he went on to tell them, "Our friend Lazarus has fallen asleep; but I am going there to wake him up."*

12 *His disciples replied, "Lord, if he sleeps, he will get better."*

13 *Jesus had been speaking of his death, but his disciples thought he meant natural sleep.*

14 *So then he told them plainly, "Lazarus is dead,*

15 *and for your sake I am glad I was not there, so that you may believe. But let us go to him."*

16 *Then Thomas (also known as Didymus[a]) said to the rest of the disciples, "Let us also go, that we may die with him."*

17 *On his arrival, Jesus found that Lazarus had already been in the tomb for four days.*

18 *Now Bethany was less than two miles[b] from Jerusalem,*

19 *and many Jews had come to Martha and Mary to comfort them in the loss of their brother.*

20 *When Martha heard that Jesus was coming, she went out to meet him, but Mary stayed at home.*

21 *"Lord," Martha said to Jesus, "if you had been here, my brother would not have died.*

22 *But I know that even now God will give you whatever you ask."*

23 *Jesus said to her, "Your brother will rise again."*

24 *Martha answered, "I know he will rise again in the resurrection at the last day."*

25 *Jesus said to her, "I am the resurrection and the life. The one who believes in me will live, even though they die;*

26 *and whoever lives by believing in me will never die. Do you believe this?"*

27 "Yes, Lord," she replied, "I believe that you are the Messiah, the Son of God, who is to come into the world."

28 After she had said this, she went back and called her sister Mary aside. "The Teacher is here," she said, "and is asking for you."

29 When Mary heard this, she got up quickly and went to him.

30 Now Jesus had not yet entered the village, but was still at the place where Martha had met him.

31 When the Jews who had been with Mary in the house, comforting her, noticed how quickly she got up and went out, they followed her, supposing she was going to the tomb to mourn there.

32 When Mary reached the place where Jesus was and saw him, she fell at his feet and said, "Lord, if you had been here, my brother would not have died."

33 When Jesus saw her weeping, and the Jews who had come along with her also weeping, he was deeply moved in spirit and troubled.

34 "Where have you laid him?" he asked. "Come and see, Lord," they replied.

35 Jesus wept.

36 Then the Jews said, "See how he loved him!"

37 But some of them said, "Could not he who opened the eyes of the blind man have kept this man from dying?"

38 Jesus, once more deeply moved, came to the tomb. It was a cave with a stone laid across the entrance.

39 "Take away the stone," he said.

"But, Lord," said Martha, the sister of the dead man, "by this time there is a bad odor, for he has been there four days."

40 Then Jesus said, "Did I not tell you that if you believe, you will see the glory of God?"

41 So they took away the stone. Then Jesus looked up and said, "Father, I thank you that you have heard me.

42 I knew that you always hear me, but I said this for the benefit of the people standing here, that they may believe that you sent me."

43 When he had said this, Jesus called in a loud voice, "Lazarus, come out!"

44 The dead man came out, his hands and feet wrapped with strips of linen, and a cloth around his face.

Jesus said to them, "Take off the grave clothes and let him go" (John 11:1-44 NIV).

Healing Bartimaeus of Blindness

"As Jesus and his disciples were leaving Jericho, a large crowd followed him. Two blind men were sitting by the roadside, and when they heard that Jesus was going by, they shouted, 'Lord, Son of David, have mercy on us!' The crowd rebuked them and told them to be quiet, but they shouted all the louder, 'Lord, Son of David, have mercy on us!' Jesus stopped and called them. 'What do you want me to do for you?' he asked. 'Lord,' they answered, 'we want our sight. Jesus had compassion on them and touched their eyes. Immediately they received their sight and followed him" (Matthew 20:29-34 NIV).

Restoring a Severed Ear

"When he rose from prayer and went back to the disciples, he found them asleep, exhausted from sorrow. 'Why are you sleeping?' he asked them. 'Get up and pray so that you will not fall into temptation.' While he was still speaking a crowd came up,

and the man who was called Judas, one of the Twelve, was leading them. He approached Jesus to kiss him, but Jesus asked him, 'Judas, are you betraying the Son of Man with a kiss?' When Jesus' followers saw what was going to happen, they said, 'Lord, should we strike with our swords?' And one of them struck the servant of the high priest, cutting off his right ear. But Jesus answered, 'No more of this!' And he touched the man's ear and healed him. Then Jesus said to the chief priests, the officers of the temple guard, and the elders, who had come for him, 'Am I leading a rebellion, that you have come with swords and clubs? Every day I was with you in the temple courts, and you did not lay a hand on me. But this is your hour—when darkness reigns'" (Matthew 20:29-34 NIV).

Chapter 31

JESUS AS THE "ANGEL OF THE LORD" IN THE OLD TESTAMENT

The very first recorded appearance of the **Angel of the Lord** was to Hagar, Abraham's mistress and the mother of his first-born son, Ishmael, *"The Angel of the Lord said to her, 'Return to your mistress, and submit yourself under her hand.' Then the Angel of the Lord said to her, 'I will multiply your descendants exceedingly, so that they shall not be counted for multitude.' And the Angel of the Lord said to her: 'Behold, you are with child, And you shall bear a son. You shall call his name Ishmael, Because the Lord has heard your affliction. He shall be a wild man; His hand shall be against every man, And every man's hand against him. And he shall dwell in the presence of all his brethren'"* (Genesis 16:9-12 NKJV).Here, the Angel of the Lord is speaking in the first person, **"I will increase your descendants, etc." This Angel of the Lord could only be Jesus!** Hagar replied to the Angel of the Lord, *"Then she called the name of the Lord who spoke to her, You-Are-the-God-Who-Sees;"* (Genesis 16:13 NKJV). Ishmael's descendants are Muslims. Several prominent Arab tribes, recognize him as an important prophet and patriarch of Islam and the forefather of Muhammad.

In another instance, the **Angel of the Lord** visited Abraham and his wife Sarah, who received a visitation at Mamre from three men. *"The Lord appeared to Abraham near the great trees of Mamre while he was sitting at the entrance to his tent in the heat of the day. Abraham looked up and saw three men standing nearby. When he saw them, he hurried from the entrance of his tent to meet them and bowed low to the ground...'Where is your wife Sarah?' they asked him. 'There, in the tent,' he said. Then one of them said, 'I will surely return to you about this time next year, and Sarah your wife will have a son.' Now Sarah was listening at the entrance to the tent, which was behind him. Abraham and Sarah were already very old, and Sarah was past the age of childbearing. So Sarah laughed to herself as she thought, 'After I am worn out and my Lord is old, will I now have this pleasure?' Then the Lord said to Abraham, 'Why did Sarah laugh and say, 'Will I really have a child, now that I am old?' Is anything too hard for the Lord? I will return to you at the appointed time next year, and Sarah will have a son.'"* (Genesis 18:1-2, 9-13 NIV). This, in the natural, would be impossible because Abraham was 100 years old, and Sarah was 90 years old, childless, and barren. The following year, Sarah did conceive her firstborn and named him Isaac. When he was a young teenager, God commanded Abraham to sacrifice the boy, in order to test his obedience, as he did Adam in the Garden of Eden. Abraham made all the preparations for the ritual sacrifice, but at the last moment, God spared Isaac. *"The Angel of the Lord called to him from heaven and said, 'Abraham, Abraham!' So he said, 'Here I am.' And He said, 'Do not lay your hand on the lad, or do anything to him; for now I know that you fear God, since you have not withheld your son, your only son, from Me.' Then Abraham lifted his eyes and looked, and there behind him was a ram caught in a thicket by its horns. So Abraham went and took the ram, and offered it up for a burnt offering instead of his son"* (Genesis 22:11-13 NKJV).

The **Angel of the Lord** also appeared to Moses in a burning bush, which did not burn up. The angel said, *"'I am the God of your father, the God of Abraham, the God of Isaac and the God of Jacob.' At this, Moses hid his face, because he was afraid to look at God"* (Exodus

3:6 NIV). Forty years later, this same angel appeared again to Moses in the wilderness of Mount Sinai in the flame of a burning thorn bush. God said, *"I am sending an angel ahead of you to guard you along the way and to bring you to the place I have prepared. Pay attention to him and listen to what he says. Do not rebel against him; he will not forgive your rebellion, since my Name is in him. If you listen carefully to what he says and do all that I say, I will be an enemy to your enemies and will oppose those who oppose you. My angel will go ahead of you and bring you into the land of the Amorites, Hittites, Perizzites, Canaanites, Hivites and Jebusites, and I will wipe them out"* (Exodus 23:20-23 NIV).

When the **Angel of the Lord** appeared to Joshua, during his battle in Jericho, he was called **Commander of the Army of the Lord,** *"Now when Joshua was near Jericho, he looked up and saw a man standing in front of him with a drawn sword in his hand. Joshua went up to him and asked, 'Are you for us or for our enemies? 'Neither,' he replied, 'but as Commander of the Army of the Lord I have now come.' Then Joshua fell facedown to the ground in reverence, and asked him, 'What message does my Lord have for his servant?' The Commander of the Lord's Army replied, 'Take off your sandals, for the place where you are standing is holy.' And Joshua did so"* (Joshua 5:13-15 NIV).When Moses was on Mount Sinai, he was also asked to remove his sandals in God's presence at the burning bush. Here, Joshua was asked to do the same thing because he was in the presence of a deity, Jesus, and not an angel. **An angel cannot accept worship**.

In each of these instances, one of the members of the Holy Trinity was depicted as the **Angel of the Lord.** He could only be God the Son because He is the one whom the Father has sent. *"I am one who testifies for myself; my other witness is the Father, who sent me"* (John 8:18 NIV).

While angels perform miracles and are given prophetic messages, there is no question that the **Angel of the Lord** in the above scriptures is not viewed as a normal angel. Especially when he was addressed as God, accepted worship, and the two people who saw "Him," thought they would die, seeing him face to face. These attributes and activities can only be attributed to Jesus, as he is distinguished from God the Father, *"No one has ever seen God, but the one and only Son, who is himself God and is in closest relationship with the Father, has made him known"* **(John 1:18 NIV).**

The **Angel of the Lord** does not make any appearances after the birth of Christ in the New Testament. Apostle John was told by an angel not to worship him, *"Now I, John, saw and heard these things. And when I heard and saw, I fell down to worship before the feet of the angel who showed me these things. Then he said to me, 'See that you do not do that. For I am your fellow servant, and of your brethren the prophets, and of those who keep the words of this book. **Worship God'"*** (Revelation 22:8-9 NKJV).

In the Old Testament, the **Angel of the Lord** is distinct and unique from all the other angels. The following scriptures describe the **Angel of the Lord** as a member of the Holy Trinity. As the Apostle John stated above, *"No one has ever seen God,"* this leaves only Jesus as the "**Angel of the Lord**" and God's messenger of the covenant in the Old Testament.

The following scriptures describe the **Angel of the Lord** as such:

Judges 6:11-14 KJV

> *"And there came an angel of the Lord, and sat under an oak which was in Ophrah, that pertained unto Joash the Abiezrite: and his son Gideon threshed wheat by the winepress, to hide it from the Midianites. **And the angel of the Lord appeared unto him, and said unto him, The Lord is with thee**, thou mighty man of valour. And Gideon said unto him, Oh my Lord, if the Lord be*

with us, why then is all this befallen us? and where be all his miracles which our fathers told us of, saying, Did not the Lord bring us up from Egypt? but now the Lord hath forsaken us, and delivered us into the hands of the Midianites. And the Lord looked upon him, and said, Go in this thy might, and thou shalt save Israel from the hand of the Midianites: have not I sent thee?"

Judges 6:21-22 KJV

"Then the angel of the Lord put forth the end of the staff that was in his hand, and touched the flesh and the unleavened cakes; and there rose up fire out of the rock, and consumed the flesh and the unleavened cakes. Then the angel of the Lord departed out of his sight. And when Gideon perceived that he was an angel of the Lord, Gideon said, Alas, O Lord God! for because **I have seen an angel of the Lord face to face."**

Zechariah 12:8 KJV

"In that day shall the Lord defend the inhabitants of Jerusalem; and he that is feeble among them at that day shall be as David; and the house of David shall be as God, **as the angel of the Lord before them."**

Judges 13:20-22 KJV

"For it came to pass, when the flame went up toward heaven from off the altar, that the angel of the Lord ascended in the flame of the altar. And Manoah and his wife looked on it, and fell on their faces to the ground. But the angel of the Lord did no more appear to Manoah and to his wife. Then Manoah knew that he was an angel of the Lord. And Manoah said unto his wife, **We shall surely die, because we have seen God."**

Judges 13:3 KJV

*"And **the angel of the Lord appeared unto the woman**, and said unto her, Behold now, thou art barren, and bearest not: but thou shalt conceive, and bear a son."*

Judges 13:8 NIV

*"Then Manoah prayed to the Lord: 'Pardon your servant, **Lord. I beg you to let the man of God you sent to us come again to teach us how to bring up the boy who is to be born.'"***

Judges 13:18 KJV

"And the angel of the Lord said unto him, Why askest thou thus after my name, seeing it is secret?"

Isaiah 9:6 KJV

*"For unto us a child is born, unto us a son is given: and the government shall be upon his shoulder: and **his name shall be called Wonderful, Counsellor, The mighty God, The everlasting Father, The Prince of Peace.**"*

2 Kings 19:35 KJV

*"And it came to pass that night, that **the angel of the Lord** went out, and smote in the camp of the Assyrians an hundred fourscore and five thousand: and when they arose early in the morning, behold, they were all dead corpses."*

Daniel 3:25 KJV

*"He answered and said, Lo, I see four men loose, walking in the midst of the fire, and they have no hurt; and **the form of the fourth is like the Son of God.**"*

It is easy to see that the **Angel of the Lord** in the Old Testament is Christ Himself. He is called God, given attributes of God, seen by people, worshiped, and distinguished from the Father and the Holy Spirit. He fulfilled prophecy.

Chapter 32
GOD CREATED MAN AS AN ETERNAL/IMMORTAL SOUL TO LIVE FOREVER

DANIEL 12:2

Eternal life begins at the moment of conception, with an individual's unequalled set of DNAs that never existed before and will never be repeated. That life has the unique combination of having a body, soul, and spirit. Upon death, only the body dies, and turns to ashes, while the spirit and soul lives on. The soul is our mental being with mind and conscience, and gives the body life. The spirit is the eternal existence of man. (see Matthew 17:1-8, Luke 16:19-31, Corinthians 5:8)

Everyone lives forever, either in heaven or hell, where time does not exist. This is because God exists apart from time. (2 Peter 3:8) To have eternal salvation, Apostle John wrote, *"He that believeth on the Son hath everlasting life: and he that believeth not the Son shall not see life; but the wrath of God abideth on him"* **(John 3:36 KJV).** To avoid his wrath, God gave his son Jesus as atonement for man's sins. Jesus accomplished this by paying the debt for all our sins, past, present, and future on the Cross of

Calvary, where he defeated Satan for the souls of mankind. Sin causes a barrier between God and man. Jesus removed that barrier when he died on the cross. **Therefore, there is no condemnation to those who repent and accept Jesus Christ as their lord and savior.**

Romans 8:2-39 KJV

"2 For the law of the Spirit of life in Christ Jesus hath made me free from the law of sin and death.

3 For what the law could not do, in that it was weak through the flesh, God sending his own Son in the likeness of sinful flesh, and for sin, condemned sin in the flesh:

4 That the righteousness of the law might be fulfilled in us, who walk not after the flesh, but after the Spirit.

5 For they that are after the flesh do mind the things of the flesh; but they that are after the Spirit the things of the Spirit.

6 For to be carnally minded is death; but to be spiritually minded is life and peace.

7 Because the carnal mind is enmity against God: for it is not subject to the law of God, neither indeed can be.

8 So then they that are in the flesh cannot please God.

9 But ye are not in the flesh, but in the Spirit, if so be that the Spirit of God dwell in you. Now if any man have not the Spirit of Christ, he is none of his.

10 And if Christ be in you, the body is dead because of sin; but the Spirit is life because of righteousness.

11 But if the Spirit of him that raised up Jesus from the dead dwell in you, he that raised up Christ from the dead shall also quicken your mortal bodies by his Spirit that dwelleth in you.

12 Therefore, brethren, we are debtors, not to the flesh, to live after the flesh.

13 For if ye live after the flesh, ye shall die: but if ye through the Spirit do mortify the deeds of the body, ye shall live.

14 For as many as are led by the Spirit of God, they are the sons of God.

15 For ye have not received the spirit of bondage again to fear; but ye have received the Spirit of adoption, whereby we cry, Abba, Father.

16 The Spirit itself beareth witness with our spirit, that we are the children of God:

17 And if children, then heirs; heirs of God, and joint-heirs with Christ; if so be that we suffer with him, that we may be also glorified together.

18 For I reckon that the sufferings of this present time are not worthy to be compared with the glory which shall be revealed in us.

19 For the earnest expectation of the creature waiteth for the manifestation of the sons of God.

20 For the creature was made subject to vanity, not willingly, but by reason of him who hath subjected the same in hope,

21 Because the creature itself also shall be delivered from the bondage of corruption into the glorious liberty of the children of God.

22 For we know that the whole creation groaneth and travaileth in pain together until now.

23 And not only they, but ourselves also, which have the firstfruits of the Spirit, even we ourselves groan within ourselves, waiting for the adoption, to wit, the redemption of our body.

24 For we are saved by hope: but hope that is seen is not hope: for what a man seeth, why doth he yet hope for?25 But if we hope for that we see not, then do we with patience wait for it.

26 Likewise the Spirit also helpeth our infirmities: for we know not what we should pray for as we ought: but the Spirit itself maketh intercession for us with groanings which cannot be uttered.

27 And he that searcheth the hearts knoweth what is the mind of the Spirit, because he maketh intercession for the saints according to the will of God.

28 And we know that all things work together for good to them that love God, to them who are the called according to his purpose.

29 For whom he did foreknow, he also did predestinate to be conformed to the image of his Son, that he might be the firstborn among many brethren.

30 Moreover whom he did predestinate, them he also called: and whom he called, them he also justified: and whom he justified, them he also glorified.

31 What shall we then say to these things? If God be for us, who can be against us?

32 He that spared not his own Son, but delivered him up for us all, how shall he not with him also freely give us all things?

33 Who shall lay any thing to the charge of God's elect? It is God that justifieth.

34 Who is he that condemneth? It is Christ that died, yea rather, that is risen again, who is even at the right hand of God, who also maketh intercession for us.

35 Who shall separate us from the love of Christ? shall tribulation, or distress, or persecution, or famine, or nakedness, or peril, or sword?

36 As it is written, For thy sake we are killed all the day long; we are accounted as sheep for the slaughter.

37 Nay, in all these things we are more than conquerors through him that loved us.

38 For I am persuaded, that neither death, nor life, nor angels, nor principalities, nor powers, nor things present, nor things to come,

39 Nor height, nor depth, nor any other creature, shall be able to separate us from the love of God, which is in Christ Jesus our Lord."

When Jesus said eternal life was knowing God, he was speaking of having an intimate, close, personal relationship with God, *"Now this is eternal life: that they know you, the only true God, and Jesus Christ, whom you have sent"* (John 17:3 NIV).

Faith comes from hearing God's Word, *"Faith comes from hearing the message, and the message is heard through the word about Christ"* (Romans 10:17 NIV). If we don't hear that Jesus came to bring us back into an intimate relationship with God, then we won't have faith in that, and we won't experience it.

Jesus wants us to have an intimate relationship with him and his father right now, in this present evil world.

When Jesus was asked by a Pharisee, who was testing him with the question, *"'Teacher, which is the greatest commandment in the Law?' Jesus replied: 'Love the Lord your God with all your heart and with all your soul and with all your mind. This is the first and greatest commandment. And the second is like it: Love your neighbor as yourself. All the Law and the Prophets hang on these two commandments'"* (Matthew 22:36-40 NIV).

Chapter 33
GOD'S FINAL WARNING TO THE WORLD: "CHOOSE LIFE OR CHOOSE DEATH"

DEUTERONOMY 30:15-20

"The Sovereign Lord never does anything until he reveals his plans to his servants the prophets" **(Amos 3:7 NLT).**

When Virginia O'Hare stood alone on the bridge, next to her home in Ft. Lauderdale, Florida, she saw and heard the thunderous speaking voice of God coming from the sky. He spoke to her these profound words, ***"Virginia, in you, I am well pleased. I have chosen you to be My last day prophet."***

This divine encounter was embraced and treasured in her spirit and soul because she knew that the spiritual gift of prophecy is an extraordinary and unique gift and should not be quenched or despised, *"Do not treat prophecies with contempt"* (1 Thessalonians 5:20 NIV). God's prophetic word is for the benefit of both believers and non-believers and is a sign that God is among his Church. He truly loves all human beings, and formed and fashioned us in his likeness and image. (Genesis 1:26-27).

God's Prophetic messages can take the form of exhortation, correction, disclosure of secret sins, prediction of future events, comfort, inspiration, or other revelations. They are spoken in human words for every human being.

GOD'S WARNING MESSAGE TO THE WORLD:

"I am God, Creator of all things in heaven and earth. I have no beginning and no end. The end of days is near. My signs and wonders are everywhere. Time is running out for mankind to repent of their sins and accept My Son Jesus as their Lord and Savior. When one takes their last breath, it will be too late to turn back to repent of their sins because the fires of hell will be waiting to engulf them for all eternity.

My thoughts are above the thoughts of all My created beings. There is no one person I love and cherish above anyone else. As I love My Son Jesus, I love all of mankind. I created all men to be equal to one another. What they become is by their own free will. I am no respecter of persons. What I will do for one I will do for everyone. Loving Me, obeying My laws, and receiving My Son as atonement for your sins, is a decision everyone must make to escape the punishment for their own sins. I've given everyone, including the angels, free will. I do not force anyone to love Me, to obey My laws, and do My will. I painfully offered My Son, Jesus, to die as an atonement for the sins of the world. I offer everyone this forgiveness and eternal life to live forever in the universe I created from the beginning. I so loved the world that I gave my only begotten son, Jesus, so that anyone who repents of their sins and believes in Him will be saved. When I created Adam and placed him in the Garden of Eden, I gave him free will and a choice not to partake of the forbidden fruit from the Tree of the Knowledge of Good and Evil. He and his wife, Eve, chose, by their free will, to disobey Me and allowed Satan, a fallen angel from heaven, to deceive them. They made the wrong choice. Satan is still tempt-

ing mankind to sin against My Commandments and Me. I have set before everyone, life, and death. I pray you will choose life!"

GOD GIVES THE CHOICE OF LIFE OR DEATH TO EVERYONE!

"See, I have set before you today life and good, death and evil. If you obey the commandments of the Lord your God that I command you today, by loving the Lord your God, by walking in his ways, and by keeping his commandments and his statutes and his rules, then you shall live and multiply, and the Lord your God will bless you in the land that you are entering to take possession of it. But if your heart turns away, and you will not hear, but are drawn away to worship other gods and serve them, I declare to you today, that you shall surely perish. You shall not live long in the land that you are going over the Jordan to enter and possess. I call heaven and earth to witness against you today, that I have set before you life and death, blessing and curse. Therefore choose life, that you and your offspring may live, loving the Lord your God, obeying his voice and holding fast to him, for he is your life and length of days, that you may dwell in the land that the Lord swore to your fathers, to Abraham, to Isaac, and to Jacob, to give them" (Deuteronomy 30:15-20 ESV).

Chapter 34

THE FINAL WAR BETWEEN GOD VS. SATAN IN THE BATTLE OF ARMAGEDDON

This generation will soon witness the greatest blood bath war of all time, between God and Satan, the Battle of Armageddon. This war will not be rivaled by all previous wars put together. The prophetic signs of this happening soon are on the horizon. According to Bible Prophesy, when Israel enters into a peace treaty, this will herald in the last seven years before the Second Coming of Jesus and the commencement of the final Battle of Armageddon. These seven years are called The Years of Tribulation. During the middle of the seven years, or at the three-and-a-half-year point, The Great Tribulation will begin. This will usher in the grand appearance of both the false prophet and the antichrist, who will rise to world power and set himself up in the Holy Temple, claiming to be God.

"So when you see standing in the holy place 'the abomination that causes desolation, spoken of through the prophet Daniel—let the reader understand — then let those who are in Judea flee to the mountains. Let no one on the housetop go down to take anything

199

out of the house. Let no one in the field go back to get their cloak. How dreadful it will be in those days for pregnant women and nursing mothers! Pray that your flight will not take place in winter or on the Sabbath. For then, there will be great distress, unequaled from the beginning of the world until now—and never to be equaled again.

If those days had not been cut short, no one would survive, but for the sake of the elect, those days will be shortened. At that time if anyone says to you, 'Look, here is the Messiah!' or, 'There he is!' do not believe it. For false messiahs and false prophets will appear and perform great signs and wonders to deceive, if possible, even the elect. See, I have told you ahead of time.

So if anyone tells you, 'There he is, out in the wilderness,' do not go out; or, 'Here he is, in the inner rooms,' do not believe it. For as lightning that comes from the east is visible even in the west, so will be the coming of the Son of Man. Wherever there is a carcass, there the vultures will gather.

Immediately after the distress of those days 'the sun will be darkened, and the moon will not give its light; the stars will fall from the sky, and the heavenly bodies will be shaken.'" (Matthew 24:15-29 NIV).

The signs that will occur just prior to this great battle are outlined in the last book of the New Testament, The Book of Revelation. All should prepare for this climactic event that will affect every single person alive, because life as we know it, will end in one hour.

"For in one hour such great riches came to nothing. Every shipmaster, all who travel by ship, sailors, and as many as trade on the sea, stood at a distance 18 and cried out when they saw the smoke of her burning, saying, 'What is like this great city?' They

threw dust on their heads and cried out, weeping and wailing, and saying, 'Alas, alas, that great city, in which all who had ships on the sea became rich by her wealth! For in one hour she is made desolate'" (Revelation 18:17-19 NKJV).

The Holy Scripture teaches that this generation will conclude with a final blood bath battle between God and Satan. The account of this final battle begins with God's sixth bowl judgment, as described in The Book of Revelation.

"Then I saw three impure spirits that looked like frogs; they came out of the mouth of the dragon, out of the mouth of the beast and out of the mouth of the false prophet. They are demonic spirits that perform signs, and they go out to the kings of the whole world, to gather them for the battle on the great day of God Almighty" (Revelation 16:13-14 NIV).

"Then I saw the beast and the kings of the earth and their armies gathered together to wage war against the rider on the horse and his army" (Revelation 19:19 NIV).

This great battle will commence by the unholy trinity of Satan, the antichrist, and the false prophet. The spirits of demons will persuade the kingdoms of the world to take part in this great battle by performing signs and wonders through the antichrist and the false prophet.

"For false messiahs and false prophets will appear and perform great signs and wonders to deceive, if possible, even the elect" (Matthew 24:24 NIV).

"And it performed great signs, even causing fire to come down from heaven to the earth in full view of the people" (Revelation 13:13 NIV).

Scripture says ten kings will have an alliance with this unholy trinity and will give their power and authority over to the beast called the antichrist.

> *"The ten horns you saw are ten kings who have not yet received a kingdom, but who for one hour will receive authority as kings along with the beast. They have one purpose and will give their power and authority to the beast. They will wage war against the Lamb, but the Lamb will triumph over them because he is Lord of lords and King of kings—and with him will be his called, chosen and faithful followers"* (Revelation 17:12-14 NIV).

> *"Then I saw the beast and the kings of the earth and their armies gathered together to wage war against the rider on the horse and his army. But the beast was captured, and with it the false prophet who had performed the signs on its behalf. With these signs he had deluded those who had received the mark of the beast and worshiped its image. The two of them were thrown alive into the fiery lake of burning sulfur. The rest were killed with the sword coming out of the mouth of the rider on the horse, and all the birds gorged themselves on their flesh"* (Revelation 19:19-21 NIV).

This war will herald in the Second Coming of Jesus Christ.

> *"Then will appear the sign of the Son of Man in heaven. And then all the peoples of the earth will mourn when they see the Son of Man coming on the clouds of heaven, with power and great glory"* (Matthew 24:30 NIV).

> *"Nothing in all creation is hidden from God's sight. Everything is uncovered and laid bare before the eyes of him to whom we must give account"* (Hebrews 4:13 NIV).

Christ will personally strike down all the nations of the world and, thereafter, rule them with a rod of iron as King of Kings and Lord of Lords.

"Coming out of his mouth is a sharp sword with which to strike down the nations. 'He will rule them with an iron scepter.' He treads the winepress of the fury of the wrath of God Almighty. On his robe and on his thigh he has this name written: KING OF KINGS AND LORD OF LORDS. And I saw an angel standing in the sun, who cried in a loud voice to all the birds flying in midair, 'Come, gather together for the great supper of God, so that you may eat the flesh of kings, generals, and the mighty, of horses and their riders, and the flesh of all people, free and slave, great and small.' Then I saw the beast and the kings of the earth and their armies gathered together to wage war against the rider on the horse and his army. But the beast was captured, and with it the false prophet who had performed the signs on its behalf. With these signs he had deluded those who had received the mark of the beast and worshiped its image. The two of them were thrown alive into the fiery lake of burning sulfur. The rest were killed with the sword coming out of the mouth of the rider on the horse, and all the birds gorged themselves on their flesh" (Revelation 19:15-21 NIV).

Those left alive will have chronic fear penetrating their entire being and want to hide.

"They called to the mountains and the rocks, Fall on us and hide us from the face of him who sits on the throne and from the wrath of the Lamb! For the great day of their wrath has come, and who can withstand it?" (Revelation 6:16-17 NIV)

The armies of heaven will be following Jesus, riding on white horses and dressed in fine linen, white and clean.

"When the Son of Man comes in his glory, and all the angels with him, he will sit on his glorious throne" (Matthew 25:31 NIV).

"The armies of heaven were following him, riding on white horses and dressed in fine linen, white and clean" (Revelation 19:14 NIV).

This war will end Satan's reign on earth, and commence Jesus's rule over the entire universe, which God created through Him from the beginning. He will reign as King of Kings and Lord of Lord forever. (Colossians 1:16)

"The seventh angel sounded his trumpet, and there were loud voices in heaven, which said: 'The kingdom of the world has become the kingdom of our Lord and of his Messiah, and he will reign for ever and ever'" (Revelation 11:15 NIV).

Chapter 35
THE REDEEMED WILL RULE AND REIGN WITH JESUS FOREVER!

Reigning with Jesus will be for all those who repented of their sins and made Jesus their Lord and Savior while they were still alive.

"This is a faithful saying: For if we died with Him, We shall also live with Him. If we endure, We shall also reign with Him. If we deny Him, He also will deny us. If we are faithless, He remains faithful; He cannot deny Himself" (2 Timothy 2:11-13 NKJV).

Every believer is called to proclaim God's word and expand his kingdom. Our rewards at the judgment seat of Christ will include our special role which our savior will give to us on that special day, where we will reign with Jesus over his creation.

"And Jesus came and spoke to them, saying, 'All authority has been given to Me in heaven and on earth. Go therefore and make disciples of all the nations, baptizing them in the name of the Father and of the Son and of the Holy Spirit, teaching them to observe all things that I have commanded you; and lo, I am with you always, even to the end of the age.' Amen" (Matthew 28:18-20 NKJV).

"I beseech you therefore, brethren, by the mercies of God, that you present your bodies a living sacrifice, holy, acceptable to God, which is your reasonable service. And do not be conformed to this world, but be transformed by the renewing of your mind, that you may prove what is that good and acceptable and perfect will of God" (Romans 12:1-2 NKJV).

God gave mankind dominion over creation to rule it for his glory.

"Then God said, 'Let Us make man in Our image, according to Our likeness; let them have dominion over the fish of the sea, over the birds of the air, and over the cattle, over all the earth and over every creeping thing that creeps on the earth'" (Genesis 1:26 NKJV).

Adam and Eve forfeited this vocation by their disobedience. Jesus Christ, as the last Adam, succeeded in reigning over God's creation. He achieved our original purpose as righteous rulers of the world.

"Therefore, just as through one man sin entered the world, and death through sin, and thus death spread to all men, because all sinned— (For until the law sin was in the world, but sin is not imputed when there is no law. Nevertheless death reigned from Adam to Moses, even over those who had not sinned according to the likeness of the transgression of Adam, who is a type of Him who was to come. But the free gift is not like the offense. For if by the one man's offense many died, much more the grace of God and the gift by the grace of the one Man, Jesus Christ, abounded to many. And the gift is not like that which came through the one who sinned. For the judgment which came from one offense resulted in condemnation, but the free gift which came from many offenses resulted in justification. For if by the one man's offense death reigned through the one, much more those who receive

abundance of grace and of the gift of righteousness will reign in life through the One, Jesus Christ.) Therefore, as through one man's offense judgment came to all men, resulting in condemnation, even so through one Man's righteous act the free gift came to all men, resulting in justification of life. For as by one man's disobedience many were made sinners, so also by one Man's obedience many will be made righteous. Moreover the law entered that the offense might abound. But where sin abounded, grace abounded much more, so that as sin reigned in death, even so grace might reign through righteousness to eternal life through Jesus Christ our Lord" (Romans 5:12-21 NKJV).

"And you He made alive, who were dead in trespasses and sins, in which you once walked according to the course of this world, according to the prince of the power of the air, the spirit who now works in the sons of disobedience, among whom also we all once conducted ourselves in the lusts of our flesh, fulfilling the desires of the flesh and of the mind, and were by nature children of wrath, just as the others. But God, who is rich in mercy, because of His great love with which He loved us, even when we were dead in trespasses, made us alive together with Christ (by grace you have been saved), and raised us up together, and made us sit together in the heavenly places in Christ Jesus, that in the ages to come He might show the exceeding riches of His grace in His kindness toward us in Christ Jesus" (Ephesians 2:1-7 NKJV).

Apostle Paul tells us our reign will also include judging the angels.

"Do you not know that we shall judge angels? How much more, things that pertain to this life?" (1 Corinthians 6:3 NKJV)

We should all be looking forward eagerly to that final day, but let us not forget that we are even now reigning with our Savior in many ways. Sin no longer has dominion over those who believe in Jesus, for we live by faith under the power of God's grace and not the law.

> *"For sin shall not have dominion over you, for you are not under law but under grace. What then? Shall we sin because we are not under law but under grace? Certainly not!"* (1 Thessalonians 5:20 NKJV)

> *"Now I say that the heir, as long as he is a child, does not differ at all from a slave, though he is master of all, but is under guardians and stewards until the time appointed by the father. Even so we, when we were children, were in bondage under the elements of the world. But when the fullness of the time had come, God sent forth His Son, born of a woman, born under the law, to redeem those who were under the law, that we might receive the adoption as sons. And because you are sons, God has sent forth the Spirit of His Son into your hearts, crying out, 'Abba, Father!' Therefore you are no longer a slave but a son, and if a son, then an heir of God through Christ"* (Galatians 4:1-7 NKJV).

By the Holy Spirit, we can now conquer sin and grow in holiness. We are also free from the tyranny of the law over guilty consciences. Forgiven in Christ, we may fulfill the royal law of liberty in serving our Creator.

> *"as free, yet not using liberty as a cloak for vice, but as bondservants of God"* (1 Peter 2:16 NKJV).

> *"But he who looks into the perfect law of liberty and continues in it, and is not a forgetful hearer but a doer of the work, this one will be blessed in what he does"* (James 1:25 NKJV).

What a glorious promise we have to look forward to. Knowing one day soon, we will sit on thrones alongside our Savior and enjoy Him and His right to rule the world. Until then, we are to refrain from sinning, bringing our mind, body, and spirit into submission to Jesus by the power of God's Holy Spirit.

Jesus will put an end to sin and death. And establish His millennial kingdom here on earth. This is the ultimate purpose of the Battle of Armageddon, to satisfy God's wrath, defeat Satan, and herald in God's Kingdom that will last forever.

> *"Behold, the day of the Lord comes, Cruel, with both wrath and fierce anger, To lay the land desolate; And He will destroy its sinners from it"* (Isaiah 13:9 NKJV).

> *"With my soul I have desired You in the night, Yes, by my spirit within me I will seek You early; For when Your judgments are in the earth, The inhabitants of the world will learn righteousness"* (Isaiah 26:9 NKJV).

> *"In those days and at that time I will cause to grow up to David A Branch of righteousness; He shall execute judgment and righteousness in the earth"* (Jeremiah 33:15 NKJV).

> *"We, according to His promise, look for new heavens and a new earth in which righteousness dwells"* (2 Peter 3:13 NKJV).

Where do you want to be when this battle occurs? You have three options. The first is to repent of your sins and be raptured by Jesus into God's kingdom, which He promised before the world began.

> *"The hope of eternal life, which God, who does not lie, promised before the beginning of time"* (Titus 1:2 NIV).

The second option is to reject God's saving grace through His Son, Jesus, and be cast into the fires of hell.

"Of how much worse punishment, do you suppose, will he be thought worthy who has trampled the Son of God underfoot, counted the blood of the covenant by which he was sanctified a common thing, and insulted the Spirit of grace?" (Hebrews 10:29 NKJV)

"and will cast them into the furnace of fire. There will be wailing and gnashing of teeth" (Matthew 13:42 NKJV).

The third option is to make no decision, which will put you on the road to hell. There, you will pay the penalty for your own sins, and be damned forever along with the multitudes.

"Let the nations be wakened, and come up to the Valley of Jehoshaphat; For there I will sit to judge all the surrounding nations. Put in the sickle, for the harvest is ripe. Come, go down; For the winepress is full, The vats overflow— For their wickedness is great. Multitudes, multitudes in the valley of decision! For the day of the Lord is near in the valley of decision" (Joel 3:12-14 NKJV).

If you have not already made the decision to accept Jesus as your Lord and Savior, say this simple prayer right now, and you, too, can be saved.

The Word of God promises everyone: *"That if you confess with your mouth the Lord Jesus and believe in your heart that God has raised Him from the dead, you will be saved"* Romans 10:9-10 NKJV

Dear Lord Jesus,

Please forgive me for all my sins. I believe You died on the cross for all my sins, and rose from the dead. I invite You to come into my heart and life, and make you my Lord and Savior. Thank You Jesus. I love You!

Amen

Now that you have prayed this simple prayer of faith. You are saved through the blood of Jesus and have eternal salvation.

God's Word in Romans 8:1-39 (NIV) confirms your salvation:

Therefore, there is now no condemnation for those who are in Christ Jesus, because through Christ Jesus the law of the Spirit who gives life has set you free from the law of sin and death. For what the law was powerless to do because it was weakened by the flesh] God did by sending his own Son in the likeness of sinful flesh to be a sin offering. And so he condemned sin in the flesh, in order that the righteous requirement of the law might be fully met in us, who do not live according to the flesh but according to the Spirit.

Those who live according to the flesh have their minds set on what the flesh desires; but those who live in accordance with the Spirit have their minds set on what the Spirit desires. The mind governed by the flesh is death, but the mind governed by the Spirit is life and peace. The mind governed by the flesh is hostile to God; it does not submit to God's law, nor can it do so. Those who are in the realm of the flesh cannot please God.

You, however, are not in the realm of the flesh but are in the realm of the Spirit, if indeed the Spirit of God lives in you. And if anyone does not have the Spirit of Christ, they do not belong to Christ. But if Christ is in you, then even though your body is subject to death because of sin, the Spirit gives life because of righteousness. And if the Spirit of him who raised Jesus from the dead is living in you, he who raised Christ from the dead will also give life to your mortal bodies because of his Spirit who lives in you.

Therefore, brothers and sisters, we have an obligation—but it is not to the flesh, to live according to it. For if you live according to the flesh, you will die; but if by the Spirit you put to death the misdeeds of the body, you will live.

For those who are led by the Spirit of God are the children of God. The Spirit you received does not make you slaves, so that you live in fear again; rather, the Spirit you received brought about your adoption to sonship. And by him we cry, 'Abba, Father.' The Spirit himself testifies with our spirit that we are God's children. Now if we are children, then we are heirs—heirs of God and co-heirs with Christ, if indeed we share in his sufferings in order that we may also share in his glory.

I consider that our present sufferings are not worth comparing with the glory that will be revealed in us. For the creation waits in eager expectation for the children of God to be revealed. For the creation was subjected to frustration, not by its own choice, but by the will of the one who subjected it, in hope that[h] the creation itself will be liberated from its bondage to decay and brought into the freedom and glory of the children of God.

We know that the whole creation has been groaning as in the pains of childbirth right up to the present time. Not only so, but we ourselves, who have the firstfruits of the Spirit, groan inwardly as we wait eagerly for our adoption to sonship, the redemption of our bodies. For in this hope we were saved. But hope that is seen is no hope at all. Who hopes for what they already have? But if we hope for what we do not yet have, we wait for it patiently.

In the same way, the Spirit helps us in our weakness. We do not know what we ought to pray for, but the Spirit himself intercedes for us through wordless groans. And he who searches our hearts knows the mind of the Spirit, because the Spirit intercedes for God's people in accordance with the will of God.

And we know that in all things God works for the good of those who love him, who[i] have been called according to his purpose. For those God foreknew he also predestined to be conformed to the image of his Son, that he might be the firstborn among many brothers and sisters. And those he predestined, he also called; those he called, he also justified; those he justified, he also glorified.

What, then, shall we say in response to these things? If God is for us, who can be against us? He who did not spare his own Son, but gave him up for us all—how will he not also, along with him, graciously give us all things? Who will bring any charge against those whom God has chosen? It is God who justifies. Who then is the one who condemns? No one. Christ Jesus who died—more than that, who was raised to life—is at the right hand of God and is also interceding for us. Who shall separate us from the love of Christ? Shall trouble or hardship or persecution or famine or nakedness or danger or sword? As it is written:

'For your sake we face death all day long; we are considered as sheep to be slaughtered.'

No, in all these things we are more than conquerors through him who loved us. For I am convinced that neither death nor life, neither angels nor demons, neither the present nor the future, nor any powers, neither height nor depth, nor anything else in all creation, will be able to separate us from the love of God that is in Christ Jesus our Lord.

Dear Reader,

I know you have been blessed by reading this God-inspired book. Please share this book with others, so they too, may be blessed and enjoy eternal life through our Lord and Savior, Jesus Christ.

Blessings,
Virginia O'Hare

Special Memorial
IN MEMORY OF ROBERT ANTHONY O'HARE

My beloved son, Robert Anthony O'Hare:
From Birth To The Battle For His Life And Justice!

An excerpt from Virginia O'Hare's best-selling book:
Virginia O'Hare Documents God's Laws Vs. Man's Laws.

ROBERT ANTHONY O'HARE

Robert Anthony O'Hare was born at St. Joseph Hospital in Elmira, NY, on November 1st, 1961. He is my third child and my only son. His birth completed our family with his two sisters Anne Marie, 3 1/2 years old, and Patty Lynne, 2 years old. When I brought Robert home from the hospital, I placed him in Patty's arms with her sister Anne Marie sitting right next to her on the sofa. I told the girls, "this is your baby brother, and you both are to take care of him." The look on their faces when they looked at their new baby brother was priceless. From that moment forward, an unbroken bond was created. The girls and their baby brother grew up with a very special closeness that lasted throughout their life. Even though the girls have gone home to be with our Lord, their spirit is still with Robert and me.

My greatest blessing was being their mother. When they were 9, 11, and 12 years of age, I became a single parent. This did not deter me from being 100% dedicated to raising my three children and working hard to support them and give them the best possible life. The details of this journey of motherhood and our life together are outlined in my first book called "Virginia O'Hare's Trials, Triumphs, and Vision from God."

Robert Anthony, Anne Marie, and Patty Lynne were very happy, gifted, and beautiful children. They each loved learning, exploring, and living life to its fullest. I began bible studies with them at a very early age. This gave them a strong foundation to guide and direct their path through life. Despite being a single parent, and working full time in my Employment Agency in Poughkeepsie, N. Y. I always placed their welfare as a priority. I instilled in them that God loves them and has a purpose for each of them and wants us to keep his Ten Commandments so we can always be blessed and live forever in Heaven with Him, Jesus, and each other. I taught them the importance of prayer. Praying together was done in our home on a regular basis, and always before every meal. Living according to God's will was a priority.

Celebrating holidays and birthday with our family, relatives, extended family, and close friends was a normal occurrence. Robert and his sisters loved getting together at Grandma's home during all these special celebrations and enjoyed the delicious home-cooked meals she made for every special holiday.

Despite the fact that Robert was the youngest sibling and got a lot of attention, he was always well adjusted and very confident within himself. His friends always followed his lead. He always exhibited a great deal of common sense, wisdom, and leadership. He was independent with a very strong, secure, and enduring character that his friends and family admired. He was very particular on how he lived his life and was very judgmental of those who weren't. His principals were always higher than most due to his being somewhat of a perfectionist about how he wanted things done.

After my divorce, I built a brand-new split-level range style home for my three children in Elmira, N. Y. This home was walking distance to their school. One day, a friend and her three children came over to our home to visit. Robert overheard me, telling her I wanted the inside of my living room repainted. He said, "mom, I can paint the walls for you." My girlfriend said, "you can't let a 12-year-old paint this beautiful home, he'll ruin it!" I looked at Robert, who was anticipating my reply, and said, "Okay, Robert, you can paint the inside of this house." His face beamed with a beautiful smile. He did a perfect professional job painting the walls. I was totally amazed.

This began Robert's painting career at an early age, as he later started working with customers from our family's very successful real estate business in Ft. Lauderdale, Fl. His services became in high demand. He would paint multi-million-dollar homes and was a perfectionist in his work. Robert excelled in doing this type of work. His referrals from past customers kept him busy and in high-demand. He made a very good living. I was amazed at his God-given talents and how many jobs he acquired just through word of mouth, and customer referrals. To say I was proud of him and my two girls would be an understatement. As they grew into adulthood, we always stayed together as a family and lived most of our lives under one roof.

From an early age, Robert had a passion for exploring for buried treasures and traveling across the country. He loved breaking their codes. He did this for 13 years and filed mining claims. He refused to sell his claims to interested buyers because he did this for the challenge and not for money.

During his treasure hunting years, he encountered baby mountain lions, snakes, and the harshness of the weather. He loved the vastness of the desert, where he was always alone. The scariest moment of his life was when he got lost in the desert and couldn't find his rented vehicle. He told me he had been exploring all day in the hot sun and was following a code he broke to a buried treasure when he lost track of time, and darkness had set in. He said he had been working and walking for miles on foot, hungry, thirsty, and exhausted and couldn't find his rented Truck. He said this was one of the most frightening experiences of his life. He had been traveling on foot all day through the harsh, barren land for several miles with very little signs of life around him other than raw, parched, dry land. He endured such challenges in his quest to find this world-famous buried treasure, "The Lost Dutchman's Mine." After filing his claims, he turned down offers to sell them for money. He said, "Mom, I didn't do this for the money. I did it for the challenge of breaking the codes." I reminded Robert that in the Bible, "God said the gold and the silver is mine, and I may give it to whomever I please."

In addition to exploring for buried treasure, Robert experimented with inventing a process to turn water into fuel. Again, he found great success with the development of the formula. He tested the product on his own vehicle, and it worked! His mind was truly blessed with God-given wisdom.

Robert never drank or smoked or took any drugs. Maintaining his mind, body, and spirit and staying in good health was always a priority to him. That's how he lived his life. He's been extremely loyal and helpful to me, his family, and friends.

After death took his two sisters and my husband home to be with the Lord, all within the span of one year and fifty-five days, Robert was an anchor to me through their passing.

Two years after their passing, a tragedy entered our life on October 5, 2015. This was the most devastating crisis both my son and I had to go through and endure. It virtually catapulted our life into a dimension that I never thought existed. The holocaust that my son was put through by the Justice System in Lake County, Florida, drove me to fight with every breath in my being to save his life and seek justice for him. It is this tragedy that gave birth to the bestselling book, "Virginia O'Hare Documents God's Laws vs. Man's Law."

ON OCTOBER 5, 2015, THREE LAKE COUNTY SHERIFF'S DEPUTIES EGREGIOUSLY VIOLATED THEIR OATH OF HONOR, ROBERT'S CIVIL, CONSTITUTIONAL RIGHTS, AND FEDERAL LAW SECTION 1983

The day began with Robert and I going through our usual morning routine in our beautiful custom-built countrified waterfront homestead property in a gated community in Mt. Dora, Florida. I was listening to my bible tapes when I heard the most blood-curdling cries I never heard before, coming from inside our home. I rushed into the living room and immediately saw three Lake County Sheriff's Deputies brutally assaulting my son. They were thrusting blunt and brutal blows to Robert's body, head, face, and eyes. Two of the Sheriff's Deputies were repeatedly kicking and punching Robert as he lay defenseless and helpless on the floor. I was in total shock, thinking this must be a nightmare. The three Deputies ignored my pleas to stop beating my son and continued their brutal assault while Robert laid helplessly on the floor crying out in severe pain!

Moments before their unlawful entry, three Lake County Sheriff's Deputies came to our home and asked Robert if they could come in the home to search for a computer, they alleged may have child porn downloaded. They said they did not have a search warrant. Robert later told me his friend in Ft. Lauderdale had given him his used laptop computer, and he was not aware that what his friend had downloaded on the hard drive was illegal. So, he told the officers to get a warrant, and he would call his attorney.

The following conversation was recorded on the Corporal's body-worn camcorder:

Sheriff's Deputy: "Anyone else here with you?"

Robert: "My Mother, can I call my lawyer?"

Sheriff's Deputy: "No."

Robert: "What did I do wrong?"

Sheriff's Deputy: "Asked for consent to come in and search the home."

Robert: "No, I want you to get a warrant!"

Sheriff's Deputy: "Step outside!"

Robert: "No."

As Robert was closing the door, the Corporal forcefully pushed open the door and stepped over the threshold of our home. He physically overpowered Robert as the other two Deputies joined in their brutal assault. That's when I walked into the room and yelled for them to stop. When they wouldn't, I ran into my bedroom and got my cell phone and began videotaping them for 35 minutes until it stopped recording.

While the first Deputy laid bodily over Robert's legs, the other two deputies, one on each side, were repeatedly kicking, hitting, and punching Robert non-stop. I kept yelling for them to stop beating my son. The second Deputy kept kicking him repeatedly on his left side, to his ribs and abdomen, soccer ball style, 10-12 times with his heavy, beige-colored work shoes while the Corporal, kneeling on one knee on Robert's right side, kept hitting him repeatedly to his head, face, and eyes. His multiple blunt blows to Robert's eyes caused a buckle (surgical drum) that had been surgically implanted a year earlier to secure a torn retina, to become wrinkled around the retina. This dislodged buckle caused Robert a severe amount of unending pain and blindness.

The second Deputy maliciously tore Robert's t-shirt down to below his chest as he drew blood on his own fist from repeatedly punching Robert's body. I later read on the police report this same Deputy lied and said Robert was running towards the kitchen, and that's why he tore his shirt. My cell phone video proved he was down on the floor just a few feet from the front entrance facing in the opposite direction of the kitchen with his t-shirt torn, exposing the severe punch marks on his neck, face, and body.

I repeatedly screamed for them to stop their beating of Robert. When they wouldn't, I ran to my bedroom to get my cell phone to record their beating. When I returned with the cell phone to record them, that's when the Deputies stopped their assault. They abruptly sat Robert upright and tightly handcuffed his wrists behind his back. Robert said the handcuffs were too tight and hurting him. I told the Deputy that his wrists were turning red while cutting off blood circulation to his hands. The officer clicked the handcuffs to an even tighter notch out of spite, which cut off the blood circulation to Robert's hands even more.

Three other law enforcement officers entered our home during this altercation, one being the Captain-in-Charge. As Robert sat handcuffed and bleeding, the Captain claimed that my son was in a tea shop in downtown Mt. Dora, with a laptop they thought had child pornography downloaded. They wanted to search the home for the laptop to inspect it. I recorded the Captain admitting **HE HAD NO SEARCH WARRANT AND NO PROBABLE CAUSE**!

They left my son sitting on the floor, his hands tightly handcuffed behind his back, cutting off his blood circulation to his hands and wrists, while they commenced searching the home for the laptop.

After searching the entire home, opening doors and drawers, and not finding the laptop, the Captain became angry. He stated, as recorded on my 35-minute cell phone video, "Even if we don't find the laptop, we are still going to arrest your son anyway."

I asked, "On what charge?"

He said, "For resisting an officer without violence."

I answered, "Resisting an officer when you forced your way into our home without a search warrant?"

Then he said, "We are going to draw up a search warrant. If we don't find the laptop, after our search, this is a free country, we will leave, but we are going to charge your son anyway with resisting an officer without violence."

The only place they did not look for the laptop was in my son's locked bedroom closet. As Robert sat on the floor, with his hands tightly handcuffed behind his back and in a beaten, traumatic and painful state, the Captain made an unlawful command to Robert, "If you don't tell us where the key is to your locked bedroom closet by the count of 10, we will kick the door off its hinges." He started counting out loud, 1,2,3,4,5,6, 7, 8, etc. Without giving his consent, Robert, in fear of reprisal, told the Captain where the key was.

The Deputies unlocked the bedroom closet door without a search warrant, without consent, without probable cause, and without any exigent circumstances, found the laptop. They removed the laptop from the closet, unzipped the case, and staged the laptop as a bogus crime scene to justify the "Plain View Doctrine." They placed the laptop on the floor and the case on the bed. Then called CSI to take pictures of their "staged" crime scene.

Evidence of the Deputies' criminal acts were recorded on their own police body-worn camcorder. They were recorded talking to each other about finding the laptop in the locked bedroom closet. The video time-stamped their conversation as being on October 5, 2015, at 11:37 a.m. They didn't have a search warrant until several hours later at 5:44 pm.

My deceased husband's firearms were in Robert's locked bedroom closet. Before his demise, he was licensed as a Florida Private Investigator and Licensed to carry firearms. Robert was charged with possession of a short-barrel rifle which the Deputies removed from his locked bedroom closet. The Detective falsely stated on the Police Report that the rifle was in "plain view." Later, under oath, this same Deputy testified at the bond hearing that he had to move clothes around the back of the locked bedroom closet to get to the short-barrel rifle. This contradicted his Police Report and his statement under oath that the rifle was in "plain view."

Witnessing my son's brutal and vicious beating by the Sheriff Deputies, and seeing his face and body bloodied and bruised, caused my blood pressure to rise to a very dangerous level. At almost 79 years of age, I was physically and emotionally feeling the adverse effects of being terrorized by the Sheriff's Deputies. The officers recognized how distraught I was and called the Emergency Medical Technicians.

When they arrived, the Deputy who punched and kicked my son repeatedly to his ribs and abdomen was the first one to meet the EMT'S at the front door asking for a band-aid for his open wound on his fist!

One EMT warned me repeatedly that my blood pressure was at a dangerously high level of 222 over 102, and said I should be immediately transported to the hospital. She gave me the tape of my blood pressure reading and stated my blood pressure was dangerously high and kept urging me to go to the hospital, or I could go into shock and die. She said, "your life is at stake." This conversation was recorded on my cell phone video.

However, hiring a criminal defense attorney for my son and safeguarding my cell phone video of the Deputies' violations took priority over dying. What good would dying do my son? My fear intensified with the thought that the Deputies would take my cell phone and erase all the evidence I had of their criminal violations. This cell phone video was the only proof I had of their brutally beating my son and conducting an illegal search and seizure of the laptop without a warrant. In addition to all their violations, I recorded the Captain's admission that they didn't have a warrant or probable cause when they entered our home. I also recorded the Corporal, who blinded my son, saying, "This happened to your son, because he wouldn't let us come in and search your home." Robert said, "Mom, they didn't have a warrant." I answered the Captain, "Without a warrant, I don't blame him for not letting you in." With all this evidence on my cell phone, I could not afford to have them take it from me and erase such legally damning evidence against all of them.

I could feel my blood pressure rising to a dangerous level, and was feeling very ill. I told the Deputies I was going to drive myself to the hospital, as suggested by the EMT. As I was leaving our home, I looked over at Robert, who was now sitting on the chair only several feet from the front entrance, traumatized by the Deputies' beating and the shock of their invasion into our home. My heart broke to leave him beaten and alone with these officers. I had to leave and drive to the hospital with my cell phone before they took it away from me. I could have died right there from a stroke just from fear alone. I needed to stay alive and focus on saving my son's life! They could have killed him with their brutal assault. Thank God, he was still alive!

While driving to the nearby Waterman Hospital, in Eustis, FL, in severe emotional pain, I focused on staying calm while praying for Robert. I needed to get him legal help as soon as possible. I left three voice mail messages to criminal lawyers I found on the internet. One lawyer called back immediately and said he had 30 years' experience in Lake County as a criminal defense attorney.

After telling him what happened, he said, "Those Deputies are doing this ass-backward. Let them take whatever they want, and I'll have it thrown out." Being told that the Deputies broke the law, I asked if he could sue them for their criminal violations. He said, "I know these Lake County Deputies personally. If I sue them, they'll plant drugs in my car. But I can get someone who can sue them for you. You are very lucky they didn't take your cell phone from you and erase the video." This attorney confirmed the Sheriff Deputies' reputation in the community who created their own standards and did not always follow the law.

After this attorney confirmed that the Deputies could take my cell phone and erase it, I detoured from going to the hospital and drove directly to Radio Shack to store my cell phone video to the cloud. On my way to Radio Shack, the second lawyer returned my call. She was from Clermont, Florida, and was a former State Prosecuting Attorney for three years and now working three years as a criminal defense attorney in her own practice. She said, "The Deputies violated your son's 4th Amendment Rights, and their acts were 100% illegal." Many months later, I met her as I was leaving the courthouse after one of my son's hearings. She remembered our conversation and reconfirmed that the acts of the Deputies were against my son's 4th Amendment Rights and were 100% illegal.

I arrived at Radio Shack and had the clerk save my video to the cloud. The third lawyer called while I was there and said he was nearby and would meet me at Radio Shack. He confirmed what the other two attorneys said, "The Deputies violated your son's 4th Amendment Rights, and this was an illegal search and seizure." All three attorneys said the Deputies could not use any of the evidence they found in my son's closet because it was "Fruit from a poisonous tree." The "fruit of the poisonous tree" doctrine is an extension of the exclusionary rule, which, subject to some exceptions, prevents evidence obtained in violation of the Fourth Amendment from being admitted in a criminal trial. Like the exclusionary rule, the fruit of the poisonous tree doctrine is intended to deter police from using illegal means to obtain evidence.

The third Attorney wanted to come back to the house with me and speak with Robert. When we arrived, Robert was still sitting in the chair by the front door, handcuffed, still in a frightened and traumatic state from his beating, covered with cuts and bruises, with his face and both eyes swollen and bruised. He said he couldn't see out of his left eye, and his abdomen and ribs were hurting him badly. He said he was in severe pain. "Mom, I'm thirsty." The officers objected to me walking into the kitchen to get him a glass of water. Even so, I returned with the water and held it up to my son's mouth, wiped his bloody wounds with several wet paper towels to clean off the blood that was still oozing from his open wounds. Robert said, "Mom, while you were away, they called CSI to take pictures of my bedroom, and they are still in there." As one of the CSI photographers was leaving, I asked her to take pictures of my son's bruised body and face for further evidence of their brutal beating. I lifted Robert's torn t-shirt so that the CSI photographer could take pictures of his wounds on his upper body, back, and chest as well as his face and eyes that were now badly swollen, bloody, and bruised.

For the next 10 hours, they had Robert sitting on a straight chair, next to the front entrance, with his hands still tightly handcuffed, while waiting for the search warrant to be drawn up. The search warrant was signed at 5:44 p.m. and delivered to our home at about 6:45 p.m. Then, two other Lake County Deputies arrived at around 10:00 pm to drive Robert to the Lake County Detention Center for booking.

I not only had to endure watching my son's vicious beating by the Deputies; I now had to witness his being taken from our home, handcuffed, with chains around his ankle and waist, and brought to the Lake County Detention Center. Robert later told me he was crammed into the back seat of their vehicle fetus style and saw the speedometer sped over 80 miles per hour as they drove him to the Lake County Detention Center.

Prior to this day, Robert never had any legal problems before these Sheriff's Deputies unlawfully forced their way into our home and literally tore our lives apart.

After Robert was taken from our home, the Captain-in-Charge went into my son's bedroom and came out holding the laptop in his hands, like it was his new-found trophy. He stated twice while holding the laptop towards me and in front of the forensic people who were sitting around the kitchen table examining the electronics, "Here look at the child porn on your son's laptop." I steadfastly refused to look at the laptop. He raised his voice and again demanded, "Here look at the child porn on your son's laptop." He was upset that I wouldn't look at the pictures on the laptop, then shouted sarcastically, "Mrs. O'Hare, you bother me!" Such disrespectful behavior coming from a Captain of the Lake County Sheriff's office was appalling, and asking me to look at child pornography was absolutely repulsive. I later learned, the Captain asking me to look at the pictures was unlawful.

After the Captain completed the investigation with the Forensic people, they all left. I later read on the Police Report that they charged my son with "Resisting an officer without violence." The Lake County Sheriff's office never filed a Use-of-Force Report. This Use-of-Force Report is required whenever the use of force is used by the officer(s) who are involved. This documentation should include a written report, photographs, collection of evidence, and recorded statements.

The U.S. Supreme Court ruled that the Fourth Amendment to the U. S. Constitution prohibits the use of deadly force to effect an arrest or prevent the escape of a suspect unless the police officer reasonably believes that the suspect committed or attempted to commit crimes involving the infliction or threatened infliction of serious physical injury and a warning of the intent to use deadly physical force was given, whenever feasible (Tennessee v. Garner, 471 U.S. 1 (1985)

In my son's case, he was not a threat. He was submissive, lying flat on the floor when the Deputies continued to use substantial and excessive police force on him. This led to the Deputies' criminal liability because Robert was in a prone position and had submitted to handcuffing. In the Rodney King case, officers used substantial force to compel King into a prone position; only the last few blows lead to criminal liability because King had complied with the order to assume a prone position and submit to handcuffing (United States v. Koon, 833 F.Supp. 769, C.D. Cal. 1993, aff'd in part, 518 U.S. 81, 1996).

The Deputies filing a charge against Robert for resisting an officer without violence in our own home was a false arrest charge. According to Florida State law and Florida Supreme Court Precedent: "A law enforcement officer may not enter a person's home to arrest them for resisting an officer without violence, even if the crime is committed in his presence, regardless of whether the suspect is in the residence when he commits that crime or commits the crime outside the residence and then flees inside." The following case laws support this Florida Supreme Court doctrine: M.J.R. v. State, 715 So.2d 1103 (Fla. 5th DCA 1998), Markus v. State, 160 So.3d 488 (Fla. 5th DCA 2015); Rodriguez v. State, 964 So.2d 833 (Fla. 2d DCA 2007), Connor v. State, 641 So.2d 143 (Fla. 4th DCA 1994), and Jackson v. State, 192 So.3d 541 (Fla. 4th DCA 2016).

In addition to the above, and just as important, the Fourth Amendment to the U.S. Constitution provides that the "Right of the people to be secure in their persons, houses, papers, and effects, against unreasonable searches and seizures, shall not be violated." Robert's 4th Amendment rights were clearly violated. The following U.S. Supreme Court case law supports this: United States v. Allen (U.S. App. Lexis 1467 2d Cir. Jan. 29, 2016). The majority opinion found that "Officers stepping across the threshold to arrest without a warrant violated the Fourth Amendment, and one's civil and Constitutional rights as well."

By midnight everyone had left. Those 12 hours were literally like going through the fires of hell. I was impacted with deep and profound emotional pain, which gripped my entire being. Not only did I lose my husband and two daughters, just two years earlier, but now seeing my son, the only living member of my family, being led off in handcuffs after being beaten and in the state of shock, was absolutely gut-wrenching. This left my heart literally pounding, aching, and broken. I went to bed, but sleep was not possible. I went back into the living room looking at the floor, reliving the terrifying nightmare of seeing my son lying there, crying out with each painful blow to his face, head, and body. To this very day, the memory of witnessing my son's beating is painfully etched in my mind and heart. I was now all alone, with dead silence surrounding me, and completely engulfed in the state of shock. I could not stop crying and praying to God, when suddenly I heard God's powerful voice in my spirit saying, "Virginia, that's how I felt when they crucified my son and nailed him to the cross." Before this moment, I never imagined the depth of God's pain and suffering as he witnessed his own son's brutal assault and crucifixion.

This scene will never diminish until I see justice for my son's life and his Constitutional rights being upheld by our judicial system. I know by the Grace of God, I will see His victory over all this evil and corruption against my son by these Lake County Deputies and the Judicial System in Tavares, Florida.

The following morning, I spoke with the Clermont lawyer again and told her what the Captain did. She said, "It was illegal for him to want you to look at child pornography. He should know better." Later that night, at around 9:00 p.m., my doorbell rang. I looked through the shutters and saw a tall Black man standing outside my front door. Not opening the door, I asked, "Who are you?"

He identified himself as being a news reporter from a local television station. I asked, "How did you get in here; this is a gated community?"

He said, "I can't say."

I told him to put his card through the mail slot in the garage door and leave.

Alone with my heart pounding with fear, I was too afraid to call the police after seeing what they did to my son. I feared the police more than I did the tall Black man standing outside my front door at 9:00 p.m.!

My husband of 45 years was a Real Estate Broker and a Florida State Licensed Private Investigator. He was also licensed to carry a concealed weapon or firearm. After he passed away, my son kept all his firearms, expensive surveillance equipment, cameras, tripods, etc. in his closet. My husband, Dan Ortung, passed away on September 31, 2013. My daughter Patricia Lynne passed away 55 days later on November 25, 2013. My eldest daughter Anne Marie passed away one year earlier on September 17, 2012. My husband and both my daughters were a total joy to my heart, as my son is and always will be.

The Lake County Detention Center said the only way I could see my son was to write him a letter asking him to permit me to visit him. I did this immediately and sent it out overnight.

ON OCTOBER 9, 2015, FOUR DAYS AFTER HIS ARREST, ROBERT'S WAS RELEASED ON BOND

On the morning of the fourth day of Robert's incarceration, a bail bondsman called and said, "Mrs. O'Hare, I'm here with your son. He is worried about you." He said he could have Robert out on bail and asked if he could come to my home for the payment of $13,500. I said, "Yes, come right over."

When he arrived, he said, "I have an attorney you can hire for your son. He is one of the ten best criminal attorneys in the state of Florida." I told him I was hiring a former prosecutor, who was coming to my home that evening. He said, "No, I'll call him right now, and he will come to your home to see you."

A few hours later, the Attorney and the bail bondsman came to my home and confirmed what the other three attorneys had said. "The Deputies' forcing their way into your home was a violation of your son's 4th Amendment Rights, and their search and seizure without a warrant were illegal. Whatever they get will be 'fruit from a poisonous tree. They cannot use it because there was no legal reason for them to force their way into your home. There were no exigent circumstances present of any crime they could see, hear, or smell, and there was no contraband in plain view. Therefore, I'm confident they will be defeated on their violating your son's 4th Amendment Rights." Both the Attorney and the Bail Bondsman stated they could have my son home that evening. On his representation that my son would be home that evening, I hired the Attorney.

Several months later, during a deposition, the Corporal who stepped over the threshold of our home without a search warrant testified that he could not view the inside of our home on October 5, 2015. He said he could not see through the shutters on the front door and windows. Therefore, he had no exigent circumstances to justify forcing his way into our home without a search warrant.

At 11:00 p.m. on October 9, 2015, the Attorney brought my son home and said, "I feel better about this case after meeting your son. He looks wholesome and is good looking and well mannered. He doesn't look anything like the charges the Deputies made against him!"

I was more than elated to see my son after his being brutally beaten by the Deputies and in jail for four days. This was the first time in his 54 years he had ever been in jail. He had no prior criminal record, lived his life as a God-fearing Christian, was self-employed as a house painter, and also worked in our family's real estate business. He never drank, smoked, or taken any drugs. My friends often told me how lucky I was to have such a good son and a close-knit family. I was proud of all three of my children. When Robert came home from the Lake County Detention Center, he said, "Mom, I prayed to God repeatedly for hours to let me come home and sleep in my own bed by 11:30 p.m." God answered my son's prayers; he was home and in his own bed by 11:30 p.m.

After bringing Robert home, our attorney advised us to leave Mt. Dora immediately and go to our other home in Ft. Lauderdale, to be safe and away from any further harm from the Lake County Deputies. He said he knew of their reputation and wanted me to leave our home as soon as possible.

We stayed at our home in Ft. Lauderdale for five months, before returning to our home in Mt. Dora to pursue a criminal complaint against the Lake County Sheriff's Department with the Internal Affairs Division

THE LAKE COUNTY CORPORAL BLINDED ROBERT IN HIS LEFT EYE

Soon after Robert was released on bond, we were able to see a Retina Macula specialist. The doctor surgically removed a scleral buckle in Robert's left eye. This buckle had been surgically implanted one year earlier to secure a torn retina. The Corporal's beating to his head and face with repeated blunt blows to his eyes caused the buckle around the retina to dislodge and wrinkle, leaving him not only blind but in constant and unending pain from the dislodged buckle.

The surgical removal of the scleral buckle relieved some of the excruciating pain Robert was experiencing, but did not restore his vision.

After several weeks of healing, we visited the Miami Eye Institute for the second surgical procedure on Robert's left eye. Unfortunately, the surgeon was unable to restore any vision to his left eye. The surgical report indicated that "Robert O'Hare's blindness was caused by a 'trauma' to his left eye," which occurred during his beating by the Corporal from the Lake County Sheriff's Office. A third surgery was to take place in the next ninety days. Due to a legal curve-ball that no one could have foreseen, new bogus charges were made upon Robert by the Lake County Prosecutor. Therefore, the third surgery was never performed, and his vision remained impaired.

During this same ten-month period of his being on bail, Robert's 6th Amendment Right to a Speedy Trial was continually blocked by the State's Prosecutor. I hired two additional lawyers for Robert, who fought hard for a Motion to Compel from the Prosecutor for their States' Discovery. In a criminal trial, the prosecution MUST release any and all evidence that it has against the defendant to his attorney. Failure to do so is a violation of the law.

Unfortunately, it is a common tactic used by corrupt Prosecutors to stall the proceedings. This led Robert's Lawyers to file a Motion to Compel Discovery. This motion is used to ask the court to order the non-complying party to produce the documentation or information requested and/or to sanction the non-complying party for their failure to comply with the discovery requests.

In Robert's case, the Prosecutor conspired with the Sheriff's Department for 300 days before the Judge issued the order to compel. This delay was an obvious violation of Robert's 6th Amendment Rights. The Judge never sanctioned the Prosecutor's failure to comply with his first Motion to Compel.

THE LAKE COUNTY SHERIFF DENIED INTERNAL AFFAIRS CRIMINAL COMPLAINT AGAINST HIS DEPUTIES AS BEING "UNFOUNDED"

Five months after leaving our Mt. Dora home and witnessing daily Robert's suffering from the Deputies' beating, I felt compelled to make a formal criminal complaint against the Sheriff's Deputies to the Lake County Internal Affairs Department in Tavares, Florida. I spoke with the Internal Affairs Investigator, who was anxious to hear the details of my complaint against the Deputies. He wanted to see me as soon as possible. I met with him and his Supervisor at their office the following day. After our meeting, they both wanted to interview my son, which happened the following day.

The next morning, the two Detectives arrived at our home. They asked Robert to tell them exactly what happened. Robert said, "Three Deputies came to our front door and asked if they could search our home. I asked if they had a search warrant? The deputy said, 'No, we do not have a search warrant.' I told them to get a search warrant, and I'll call my lawyer. As I was closing the door, the three deputies forced the door open, entered our home, punched me in the stomach, knocked me to the floor, then one officer started kicking me repeatedly 10-12 times to my ribs and stomach on my left side. The other officer, on my right side was on his knees repeatedly cuffing me to my head, face, and eyes. I could not see out of my left eye. He blinded me! The third deputy was bodily, holding down my ankles while the other two officers, on each side of me, kept beating me. I was in terrible pain. My mother walked into the room and was yelling at them to stop beating me. They wouldn't stop hitting and kicking me." My son asked if they would take a lie detector's test on him and the Deputies because he said, "I'm telling the truth."

The Internal Affairs Department continued to investigate my criminal complaint and eventually interviewed all the Deputies that were in our home on October 5, 2015. In the official Internal Affairs report, one of the Deputies swore under oath, "We thought going into the defendant's home (O'Hare) without a warrant would work like it did all the other times." In other words, these Lake County Sheriff's Deputies made it a practice to violate the law anytime they could get away with it. Internal Affairs never had the Deputies take a lie detector's test.

A full investigative Lake County Internal Affairs report was given to the Prosecutor for his review. Instead of acknowledging the evidence in the report against the Deputies' criminal violations to Robert's 4th Amendment rights and Federal Statute 42 U.S.C. § 1983, he ignored all this evidence from the Lake County Internal Affairs criminal investigation report and conspired with the Deputies to create even more damning lies and false allegations against Robert to cover up his prosecutorial misconduct and the Deputies' violations.

The State Prosecutor was given a copy of this criminal report and failed to act on the Deputies' violations as well as the Lake County Sheriff. He dismissed the criminal complaint against the Deputies as being "unfounded."

SECOND "BOGUS" ARREST CHARGE FILED AGAINST ROBERT ON AUGUST 17, 2016

Wednesday, August 17, 2016, started out the same way most days did. Robert had been out on bond for a little over ten months, and we were living in our second home in Bay Colony, a small, upscale, gated waterfront community in Ft. Lauderdale, FL. We left our home around noon to run a few errands and have lunch. We were about to pull on to the street when I noticed a large, dark blue SUV starting to tailgate us very closely. We had no idea who this was, and I feared that they might hit our vehicle.

I told Robert to drive down the next dead-end street to see if the vehicle would follow us. It not only followed us but drove past us and made a U-turn at the end of the cul-de-sac street, then sped head-on towards our car. To avoid a head-on collision, Robert immediately turned our car to the right side of the road and stopped just over the swale of our neighbor's lawn to avoid a head-on collision. Just then, another vehicle came speeding down the street towards our stopped car and smashed his large SUV into the passenger's side of our vehicle. The driver jumped out of his vehicle, pointed his gun at us with his arms shaking nervously back and forth. Then, for no reason, he used a sharp iron instrument and smashed the rear window of our parked car, splattering glass all over the inside of the car.

Just then, several other cars came onto the street, also unmarked with no lights or sirens. Then a voice command came from the first vehicle that was tailgating us, "Put your hands up in the air!" Robert immediately put his left hand up over his head, at the officer's command, while keeping his right hand on the stick shift, while trying to put it in a park position. The stick shift was stuck and difficult to put into the park position due to the impact of the officer's large SUV driving onto the back wheel on the passenger's side of our vehicle. A mechanic later informed me that the vehicle smashing into the rear tire bent the axle, which made it difficult for Robert to move the stick shift to the park position. Robert said, "The stick shift is stuck!" After several tries, Robert finally got it into the park position.

The U. S. Marshal told Robert to get out of the car and lie flat on the pavement. Robert unfastened his seat belt and laid face down on the hot pavement. When he did this, one of the Police Officers abruptly pulled Robert's right arm up in the air, lifting him bodily off the pavement, then dropped him flat on his face on the concrete pavement. From this officer's brutal act, Robert landed face down, scratching his face, arms, and knees on the hot pavement with his left arm underneath his chest. Just then, the other officer laid across Robert's left shoulder and said, "Put your hands behind your back." Robert put his right hand behind his back, but with the officer's full body weight laying on Robert's left shoulder and his left arm underneath his chest, it was difficult to do this. I heard the officer yelling, for no reason, "Stop resisting, stop resisting." Robert was not resisting! He was lying flat on the pavement.

Despite the pain he was in, Robert forced his left hand from underneath his chest, with the weight of the officer still on his shoulder, causing his arm and hand to be scratched and bloodied from the concrete pavement. He did this to comply with the officer's command. I took pictures on my cell phone that shows cuts and bruises with blood on his arm, face, hand, and knees while complying with the officers' command to put his left arm behind his back. He never once resisted the officer without violence as the Officers falsely charged.

Instantly, my mind flashed back to the scene of the Lake County Deputies brutally beating my son on October 5, 2015, and falsely accusing him of resisting an officer without violence, and now watching another incident of the brutal police force being used on him was very devastating. I yelled and said, "He is not resisting! He can't get his hand behind his back with your 200 lbs. of body weight laying on his shoulder. I'm going to sue you for using excessive force on my son and crashing into my parked car." When I later lodged a complaint against this officer, I was told this was his first week on the job.

The U.S. Marshal said he had a warrant from Lake County. I asked him for a copy of the warrant. He replied, "I don't have a copy of the warrant."

I immediately called our attorney on my cell phone and had him speak with the U.S. Marshal in charge. He told our attorney, "We are charging Robert with resisting an officer without violence because we used force." The officer admitted they were the ones who used force, not Robert, yet they charged him with resisting an officer. They filed the false charge of resisting an officer without violence, to justify their using excessive police force on my son, and smashing into my car, then breaking out the back window.

We later received a sworn affidavit from the U.S. Marshal, stating that the fact they used force during the arrest is enough of a reason to charge Robert with "Resisting an officer without violence." This fabricated charge invalidated my son's $25,000 bond in Lake County that I paid for, four days earlier.

As they were putting Robert into their vehicle, he informed them that he was experiencing extreme intestinal pain and was suffering from painful intestinal bleeding problems. The U.S. Marshals took my son to the Emergency Room at the Broward Health Medical Center in Ft. Lauderdale, Florida, for observation. The Broward Health medical report stated that my son had pre-cancerous bleeding polyps and should be seen by a Gastro-Intestinal (GI) Doctor within three days and must have a colonoscopy

After they took Robert away, one of the officers drove my car back to my home because it was unsafe for me to drive after the officer crashed into it with his SUV. I had a mechanic pick up my car to repair the body damage. That's when I learned the rear axle was bent and unsafe to drive. The expense of fixing the axle caused me to trade it for a new car.

Upon being released from the Broward Health Medical Center, Robert was taken to the Paul Rein Detention Facility in Pompano Beach, FL. However, because of the revocation of his bond in Lake County, he was soon transferred back to the Lake County Detention Center.

Our legal team, which had grown to four attorneys, were now forced to continue fighting the prosecutorial misconduct in Lake County while the Broward Lawyer was preparing for a trial in Broward County on the false charge of "Resisting an officer without violence."

THE LAKE COUNTY PROSECUTOR'S PROSECUTORIAL MISCONDUCT CONTINUED UNABATED

At this point, Robert's tragic story becomes elevated and twists into so many different catastrophes.

First, because of Robert's second arrest on August 25, 2016, to revoke his bond, due to his false resisting charges by the U. S. Marshal, he was not able to receive the third surgery to attempt to restore vision to his left eye, leaving Robert with impaired vision.

Second, the Lake County Prosecutor deliberately stalled our Forensic Attorney for five months before allowing him to examine the State's Forensic Report. Keeping Robert incarcerated and suffering without any medical treatment for his malignant colon cancer

Third, the Prosecutor delayed sharing requested Discovery Files with the defense for ten months. He even ignored the first Motion to Compel order from the Judge, and it was only with a second Motion to Compel issued by the Judge that the State Attorney's office finally turned over the required documents to the defense. This delay was a violation of his constitutional due process.

Fourth, the new charges of "Resisting an officer without violence" filed by the U.S. Marshals Service in Broward County triggered the revocation of his bond in Lake County. This caused Robert to be incarcerated without the benefit of medical treatment for his impaired vision and treatment for his malignant colon cancer. Plus, due to those bogus charges, there were additional legal fees for Robert's representation of these charges.

Without question, the second charges by the Prosecutor were issued in vindictive retaliation for my filing a criminal complaint with the Lake County Internal Affairs Division. There was no new evidence against Robert, only the Prosecutor's vivid imagination of the same evidence they collected during the warrantless search of our home on October 5, 2015. His second arrest charges falsely stated that Robert delivered two "toy" Jukeboxes to a neighbor in 2011 or 2012 with lenses in them for spying. The Prosecutor admitted to a news reporter that he assumed Robert deliberately delivered these toys to the wrong addresses so that the homeowners would think that a package had simply been misdelivered and that they would bring the package to the correct neighbor, a few doors down.

The ridiculous assumption by this Prosecutor never had any evidence whatsoever that Robert delivered anything to anyone, let alone two toy jukeboxes. The Prosecutor released this false story to the press, and it was picked up and spread by media outlets around the world. The Prosecutor admitted to the media that he had merely "ASSUMED" Robert delivered the jukeboxes and thus filed the charges on his assumption theory.

The Prosecutor carried this story even further when he CON-SPIRED with a Detective from the Lake County's Sheriff's Office to LIE IN COURT under oath that he received information from a Broward County Officer that Robert delivered two empty juke-boxes to a family in Broward County. Under oath, he gave the name of the Broward Officer, who I just happened to know. This Broward Officer was the one who smashed his SUV into my parked car and broke the back window out with his gun. It was this Officer who pointed his gun at Robert and me when they served the warrant for his arrest. It was this Officer who laid bodily on Robert's left shoulder and lied and said Robert was resisting an Officer without violence. During the trial for these bogus charges, it was this Officer that lost the verdict, and it was Robert who won the verdict of being Not Guilty. It was this Officer who left the Broward Courtroom with his tail between his legs.

I made a brand-new complaint against this Broward County Officer to Internal Affairs in Ft. Lauderdale, Fl, regarding the sworn statement made by the Lake County Detective, who falsely swore under oath he was told by this Broward County Officer that Robert gave two empty Jukeboxes to a family in Broward in 2016. I did this so I would have the evidence to bring back to Lake County Judicial System. I knew first hand this Lake County De-tective was committing PERJURY, which I later proved. Both the Broward Sargent and Internal Affairs Investigator in Ft. Lauder-dale, Fl., stated Officer xxxx NEVER MENTIONED ROBERT DE-LIVERED TWO EMPTY JUKEBOXES TO A FAMILY IN 2016, to the Lake County Detective. This was further confirmed by the ac-tual Broward County Police Report in which there was no mention of any Jukeboxes being delivered by Robert. The Lake County De-tective fabricated this bogus statement under oath during Robert's Bond Hearing and caused the judge to deny reinstatement of his $25,000 bond.

Upon receiving this lethal information against the Lake County Detective, I filed a complaint with the Lake County Internal Affairs about this Detective committing Perjury at Robert's Bond Hearing. The Lake County Internal Affairs Investigator chose to dismiss the findings of the Broward County Internal Affairs investigation, and no charges were brought against the Lake County Detective for lying under oath against my son and committing perjury. His lie caused the Judge to deny reinstatement of my son's $25,000 Bond, which further delayed treatment for Robert's growing colon cancer.

Before Robert's trial in Broward County for the resisting charges, his Attorney was in pre-trial negotiations with the Broward County Prosecutor to drop the resisting charges. He said they were making headway towards the charges being dropped for Robert's bond to be reinstated in Lake County, so he could be released and have urgently needed medical treatment for his colon cancer. The Lake County Prosecutor, who conspired with the Lake County Detective to lie about the Broward Officer, now was trying to vindictively sabotage my son's chance for having the charges dropped. He called the Broward County Prosecutor and told her that Robert was a flight risk and a danger to the community. He sent her an audio recording of one of my conversations with my son during one of our monitored jail calls.

The Broward County Prosecutor said she wanted to meet with me before making her decision. Knowing the reinstatement of my son's bond was predicated upon her dropping those resisting charges in Broward County, I was more than pleased to have the opportunity to meet with her and give her my eyewitness account of the events of the U.S. Marshals' false resisting charges.

During this meeting, she told me about the call she had received from the Lake County Prosecutor. She said after she listened to his audio, she would let my attorney know of her decision.

She said, "I heard you read some of the new book that you're writing while you spoke to your son on the jail phone. I wanted you to continue reading more of it. It sounded very interesting. You must have done a lot of research for the book. I want to purchase it when it comes out."

She asked what the name of the book would be. I told her, "Virginia O'Hare Documents God's Laws vs. Man's Laws." She also wanted the name of the first book I had published a year earlier. I told her, "Virginia O'Hare's Trials, Triumphs, and Vision from God." She said she wanted to purchase that book as well. I told her both books were written and inspired by God's Holy Spirit, with Divine warnings of disasters coming upon our generation, with the end of days just around the corner!

On the audio she was given by the Lake County Prosecutor, I was recorded as saying, "Robert, when this is over, we are going to travel around the world." Robert's response was, "My preference is to ride my motorbike through the Blue Ridge Mountains."

That recording was taken completely out of context. She opted to ignore all the evidence submitted to her during her pre-trial negotiations with our attorney and went with the Lake County Prosecutor's false characterization of Robert being a flight risk and a danger to the community. I told her, through tears, "you will lose this case when it goes to trial!"

Her decision meant that Robert would be denied bail on the "resisting" charges and remain in custody at the Lake County Detention Center. This would result in Robert's first bond for $13,500, stemming from the original arrest on October 5, 2015, being revoked, and Robert's second bond for $25,000 for the 2nd charge on August 17, 2016, being revoked as well.

On November 9, 2016, Robert was transported back to Ft. Lauderdale for his scheduled trial date set in Broward County for the "Resisting an officer without violence charge.

On November 8, 2016, both the Prosecutor and Robert's Attorney found the prospective jurors to be totally unacceptable and blocked all the jurors. The new trial date was rescheduled for November 29th, 2016, to pick a new set of jurors. This meant that Robert would return to the Paul Rein Detention Center in Pompano Beach, FL, for the next three weeks awaiting the new trial date. For the first time in his 55 years, Robert would spend Thanksgiving in Paul Rein Detention Center. For his Thanksgiving meal, Robert was given four slices of white bread with baloney. This was one of the regular meals on the inmate's lunch menu.

On the morning of November 29, 2016, I drove to the Broward County Courthouse, anxious to see my son for the first time since he was incarcerated on August 25, 2016. I was blessed with a parking space right next to the courthouse building and had only a few minutes to get to the courtroom on the 4th floor before the trial began. When I stepped out of my car onto the sidewalk in front of the courthouse, I accidentally tripped on a broken protruding edge of the sidewalk. I fell on my hands and knees with copies of legal papers for my son's trial flying in all directions from the gusty winds. Retrieving all the documents alone was impossible. The papers were blown in several different directions. Hurting badly from the fall, I got up and tried to get as many of the documents as I could. A lady and a man came to my rescue and ran to gather up every single document.

I hurried into the courthouse with my papers all disarranged, but every document back in my folder. I stopped in the restroom to clean my wounds before going into the courtroom. The Broward County Prosecutor came into the restroom and said, "Did your attorney call and tell you the trial has been canceled again and rescheduled." My heart sank as I was trying to catch my breath after the fall and rushing to be on time for Robert's trial.

Disappointed, I asked, "To when?"

She said, "I don't want to tell you."

I asked, "Please!"

She said, "To January 24, 2017."

I asked, "Why?"

She said, "Because your attorney was too sick with the flu to try your son's case."

I thought, "This cannot be happening!" I was bloody with bruises on my hands and knees, trying hard to hold back the sadness of not being able to see my son and dealing with the pain from the fall.

The Prosecutor said, "Let's sit on a bench in the hallway." We spoke for about a half-hour.

I asked her, "Why are you doing this to my son? You have all the evidence you need to prove my son was not resisting those officers. Those lying officers have caused my son to lose his bond!"

Her answer was, "I'm just doing my job."

This delay meant I would spend Christmas and New Year's Eve alone without my son, the only living member left of my family. Fortunately, my friends invited me to celebrate the holidays with their family for lunch, and other friends invited me to dinner with their family members.

I spoke almost daily to my son during the ten weeks he was incarcerated at the Paul Rein Detention Center while waiting for his new trial date. On a positive note, the Paul Rein Detention Center is a far superior facility and more humane than the Lake County Detention Center. It has no bars, only doors on the dorm-like rooms that housed the inmates. This facility offered sports activities, bible studies, and Robert was allowed to go outside daily in the fenced yard. It is a very well operated facility. I met three times with the nursing administrator to let her know of my son's precancerous bleeding colon polyps to coordinate his medical treatments. She said their facility scored 100% by the State of Florida for the operation of their facility. After reviewing Robert's medical reports from the Broward Health Medical Center Report and two letters from two GI specialists, she said she would do everything she could to get Robert a GI Doctor as soon as possible.

I prayed with my son daily during our monitored jail calls. I put extra money for Robert in his account for commissary orders, so he could buy what he needed and give to the other inmates who were not so fortunate. He did this regularly. He told me how much they appreciated this because they did not have the funds to buy from the commissary and were tired of eating the same meals, with no variations in the menu.

One night at 8:00 p.m., Robert called me and said, "Mom, put on your bathrobe, we're going for a walk down our street as we used to every night when I was home." Surprised and happy, I put my bathrobe over my nightgown and walked outside while talking with my son on my cell phone. I was blessed with our ongoing conversations, which were always on world events, especially current breaking news and Bible prophecy. Even though I walked alone down the street then back to our two-story colonial home, I could actually feel his presence being there with me even though we were only talking on the phone. After that, we did this on a regular basis. These walks were truly a blessing and a joy for me to take while talking with Robert on the monitored jail phone.

We never ran out of conversations. We all loved keeping abreast of world affairs and tying them together with Bible prophecy. One evening while we were talking on the phone, and I was walking alone down our street, Robert asked me, "Mom, look up at the stars in the sky. Do you see the moon and the three bright stars next to it?"

I said, "Yes, Rob, I do."

"That's good because I can see the same from my third-floor cell window, the moon, and the three stars." Then he said, "Because it is New Year's Eve, I want you to go to the Pompano Isles Buffet tomorrow." My husband, and my daughters and I often dined there. Coincidentally, friends invited me to join their family to celebrate New Year's Day with them at Pompano Isles Buffet. Other dear friends invited me to their home that evening for a home-cooked dinner. My son was happy to hear I was going to our favorite restaurant, and we both knew that God orchestrated the entire holiday. Robert said, "Just because I'm suffering in here doesn't mean you have to as well."

The third rescheduled jury trial in Broward County commenced on January 24, 2017. Seeing my son for the first time, since his arrest on August 25, 2016, was heart-wrenching. He was led into the courtroom with chains around his hands, waist, and ankles. His body looked thin, frail, and sickly. His cheekbones protruding from his face showed the excessive amount of weight he lost during his first and only time in his life of being incarcerated. His colon cancer was taking a toll on his health, and no proper medical treatment was given to him by the Detention Centers. As a mother, witnessing all this ongoing corruption in the Lake County Judicial System, and now my son having to face these false charges against him by the Broward County Officers, was disturbing to the core of my being.

During the two-day jury trial in Broward County, the three U.S. Marshals nervously testified with inconsistent stories to support their false charges of "Resisting an officer without violence." The Broward County Prosecutor, without any credible evidence, tried to defend and support the three lying U.S. Marshals' testimony. She was sorely losing the battle to convince the Jurors and the Judge. This Broward County Judge was honorable, decent, and fair. He followed the law to the "T." The Lake County Judge was just the opposite. He was biased, unfair in his rulings, and did not follow the law.

When I took the stand and testified as an eyewitness that my son was not resisting the officer, and was only compliant, the Prosecutor tried in vain to "impeach" my testimony. She took the evidence she had received during the pre-trial negotiations with Robert's lawyer and tried to present it to the Judge. Our attorney objected, saying that according to the rule of law, it is not permissible to take evidence submitted during pretrial negotiations into a court of law. He added, "I'm surprised that she would do such a thing; she knows better."

The Judge overruled her motion to impeach my testimony. Despite overruling her and allowing my testimony to stand as an eyewitness for my son, she kept insisting I be impeached. She wanted the Judge to hear my taped conversation with my son that was provided to her by the Lake County Prosecutor and taken completely out of context. The Judge dismissed the jurors and me from the courtroom and listened to the taped conversation. My son later told me that after the Judge heard the taped conversation, he scolded the Prosecutor and said, "Did you not hear what I said, 'Overruled!' Stop badgering this 80-year-old woman. I'm not changing my ruling. You are not going to impeach her as a witness!"

I went back into the courtroom and finished my testimony as an eyewitness to the U.S. Marshal's false charge that my son resisted an officer during their arrest. After that, my son testified and told the Jurors exactly what happened, which was supported by all the prima facie evidence. Shortly after that, the jurors left the courtroom for deliberation.

During the two-day trial, the jurors listened carefully and reviewed all the evidence presented to them: (1) Testimony of the three U.S. Marshals, (2) Robert's testimony, (3) My eyewitness testimony, (4) Pictures of the police inflicted wounds on my son's face, neck, arms hands, and body, (5) Pictures of the officer's SUV after smashing into my car on the passenger's side, and breaking the back window, (6) The cost of repairs and replacement for my damaged vehicle, and (7) Our attorney's sworn statement from the U.S. Marshal's admission to him stating, "Because we used force, that's why we charged Robert with resisting an officer without violence." With all this evidence, the jury returned after less than 10 minutes of deliberation, with a verdict in favor of my son, "Not guilty."

After the Broward County Jury came back with a "not guilty" verdict, the Prosecutor came over to me and said, "Congratulations! I wish you and your son peace; I know you both have been put through hell!" I deeply appreciated her kind and heartfelt words.

My son and I were elated over the verdict. I thanked God and complemented our Broward Attorney for a job well done. He said, "Don't thank me; I didn't win this case for your son. Your son won his own case by telling the whole truth most thoroughly, with all the details that were supported by the evidence. Your son was most eloquent!" I, too, was impressed and proud of Robert's testimony, and his incredible strength of character living through and triumphing over the false charge made by the three U.S. Marshals.

Only God could give such strength and endurance for Robert to live through all these serious violations committed against him by Law Enforcement Officers in both Lake County and Broward County. Fortunately, my son had his day in court, and the Judge and Jury in Broward County ruled in his favor against the lying U. S. Marshalls.

Several months later, I was in a restaurant located by the Ft. Lauderdale Inter-coastal Waterway. I was having lunch with my friend, a Senior Vice President of a local bank. We were enjoying our meal and celebrating our 30-year-old friendship when the former Broward County Prosecutor came over to our table. She hugged me and said, "You don't know how often I think of you. In fact, I think about you all the time. I'm a mother of a son and can identify with what you are going through."

She wanted to know how my son and I were doing. I told her, "Keeping our faith in God!"

She said, "I don't hug anyone, but I am hugging you."

I reminded her, "I told you my son was going to win his case."

My friend told the Prosecutor, "Virginia was born with a gift of seeing things before they happen and is 100% accurate."

We wished each other well. The meeting was a fine moment of closure for both of us.

The U.S. Marshal's false charges of resisting an officer without violence caused my son to go through all these dreadful experiences, including being ostracized from our upscale gated community. The U.S. Marshal's arrest of Robert on August 17, 2016, was made in Bay Colony, the small, upscale, gated community on the waterfront in Ft. Lauderdale, FL, where we had maintained a second residence since 2011.

The U.S. Marshal's method of arresting Robert with violence and filing their false charge against Robert led the lawyer for the homeowner's association to forbid my son to reside in our community because his arrest was considered a "nuisance," which is not allowed in the By-Laws.

This issue faded away immediately when my son was found innocent of the charges by a Broward County Jury. In fact, the Captain of the Guards, said to me, "Virginia, with your faith in God, I know that Robert will be free and home with you soon. I'm praying for you both." The Association asked me to run for one of their offices. I declined so that I could devote my time to exonerating my son from those horrible bogus charges in Lake County, Florida.

The financial expense to defend Robert against the U. S. Marshal's false charge of "Resisting an officer without violence" was not only costly but damning to my son's case in Lake County. It gave the Lake County Prosecutor a foothold to incarcerate my son for 24 months without a bond.

The following are some of the financial damages caused by this false charge of Resisting an Officer without violence by the U. S. Marshals: legal fees for Robert's lawyers to handle the Broward County Case $17,500; replacement cost of a new car with the trade-in $15,000, and the loss of both Bonds of $13,500 and $25,000 respectively. Worst of all, even more than the financial damages are the 24 months of torturous incarceration in Lake County and Marion County Detention Facilities without receiving any urgently needed medical treatment for his malignant stage 4 colon cancer. Both these facilities are under the supervision of State Attorney Brad King.

After winning a "Not Guilty" jury verdict in Broward County on January 26, 2017, Robert's lawyers were hopeful that the Lake

County Judge would now reinstate his bond in Lake County because he had no LEGAL reason not to.

After winning the Jury Verdict in Broward County, Robert was transported back to the Lake County Detention Center to await his Motion to Reinstate his bond. This was the day before he was scheduled to see the GI Doctor in Paul Rein Pompano Beach Detention Center. Missing the medical appointment with a GI Doctor was a major disappointment. Yet, we were hopeful the Lake County Judge would do the right thing and reinstate Robert's Bond. Especially after a Broward Jury exonerated him from the U. S. Marshal's false charge of resisting an Officer.

During my son's Bond Hearing on February 24, 2017, the Lake County Prosecutor lied to the Judge and said Robert was a danger to the community and a flight risk, and his bond should not be reinstated.

The Judge asked me about this. I said, "Your honor, I told my son, when this is all over, I want us to travel around the world. This is something that I've always wanted to do but never did in my 80 years of life. Those were not Robert's words, but mine. I was trying to comfort my son with this to look forward to. He is not a flight risk."

The Prosecutor purposefully had taken our monitored jail calls completely out of context in front of the Judge and never produced any evidence to support his false allegations.

The Prosecutor didn't stop there with his character assassination on my son. He called, as his "star" witness, the Deputy who brutally and viciously assaulted my son during his unlawful warrantless entry into our home on October 5, 2015.

When the Prosecutor questioned this Deputy about listening

to my conversations with my son on our monitored jail calls, Robert's trial Lawyer attorney immediately objected to the Deputy giving a third-party hearsay testimony, without first producing the jail phone calls. The Judge ordered the Prosecutor to give a copy of the phone calls between my son and me to Robert's attorney. The hearing was canceled and rescheduled for the following month. This delay caused my son to have to wait still another month without any medical treatment for his pain and suffering from stage 4 colon cancer. He was dealing with the constant issues of dealing with intestinal bleeding and severe bowel problems as a result of the tumor that was blocking his colon 70%. I looked over to my son, who was pale and sickly looking with the loss of weight, showing on his face and entire body with the excessive loss of weight. He took a deep breath of disappointment that this would delay his medical treatment for yet another month.

As the Deputy exited the courtroom, he walked past me, wearing the same beige shoes he wore when he brutally and repeatedly kicked my son in his stomach and ribs. I thought, "Dear God, how do we fight against all this corruption, conspiracy, bias, and injustice against my son?" God's powerful words to my spirit were, "Virginia, no weapons forged against your son will prosper, and there will be a judgment on those who did this to him."

Prior to the next Bond Hearing on March 20, 2017, the Lake County Prosecutor told Robert's lead Attorney, "I'm going to put your client away for life." After the Bond hearing, the Lead Attorney told me, "Virginia, your son was set up at the Bond Hearing by the Prosecutor and Deputies. You need to immediately hire a Civil Rights Attorney to save your son's life."

At the rescheduled Bond Hearing, the Prosecutor never brought up the taped jail phone conversations between my son and me because he knew he took those conversations out of context. With the taped conversation, he could not prove his false allegations. He didn't have his star witness, the Deputy who beat my son, testify either. However, he did have two neighbors from our Loch Leven community testify.

The first neighbor said, "I saw Robert taking walks at 9:00 p.m. with his mother on the street in front of their home.

The other neighbor said, "I close my shades at night for privacy.

From these two statements, the Lake County Prosecutor convinced the Judge that my son was a "danger" to our neighborhood. Later, the Prosecutor told Robert's lead Attorney, "I let Mrs. O'Hare's neighbors listen to her jail calls with her son.

The Prosecutor could see that any hearsay evidence presented a month earlier and the testimony of these two neighbors was not going to be enough to convince the Judge to continue to deny bail. He needed something "big" to keep Robert from being released on bond. He wanted to prevent any evidence about the illegal, warrantless search by the Deputies and the excessive, brutal force they used against Robert from coming out, which would destroy his entire case against convicting Robert.

The Prosecution's next witness was a Lake County Sheriff's Detective. The Prosecutor had conspired with this witness to lie under oath and create a story that would paint Robert as a danger to the community. during his testimony, the Detective falsely stated, "I was told by Broward County Officer Brian Schaeffer that Robert O'Hare delivered two jukeboxes to a family in Broward County, FL In 2016." I saw Robert, shaking his head in total disbelief at this false statement coming from the Detective.

The main purpose for the Prosecutor having the Detective make this bogus statement up at the Bond hearing was to support his own false charges made seven months earlier in which he falsely accused Robert of delivering two Jukeboxes to a family in our subdivision in 2011 or 2012. The Prosecutor wasn't even sure which year his made-up story was in. He gave this bogus story to the news media, stating that he assumed Robert had delivered two Jukeboxes to the wrong neighbor thinking the wrong neighbor would deliver the Jukeboxes to the right neighbor. He spread his "assumption theory" to the news media, which was spread all over the country and is now permanently registered on the worldwide internet.

The Prosecutor's collusion with the Lake County Detective was to create another "Jukebox Story" to support his own "Jukebox Story" to justify his second arrest charges against Robert. Ironically, I had dealt with this Broward Officer personally at the scene of the 2nd arrest on August 17, 2016. I had filed a complaint against him to his supervisor and Internal Affairs. So, I knew who Detective xxxx was referring to.

During a court recess, I asked Robert's Attorney, "If I can prove that Detective xxxx lied about the Broward County Officer telling him that Robert gave two jukeboxes to a family in Broward County in 2016, what would that do?" The Attorney said, "If he lied about something like that under oath, that would be lethal against the Detective."

To get the necessary evidence I needed to prove Detective xxxx was lying under oath about his bogus Jukebox story, I filed another formal complaint with Internal Affairs against the Broward Officer xxxx. He testified that he never said Robert gave two jukeboxes to a family in Broward County in 2016. His Sargent further added, "We don't have any Jukeboxes on our police report as proof of this. You have a copy of that Police Report, you can see for yourself there are no jukeboxes reported. If that jukebox story were true, it would have to be put on the Police Report. We just don't make up stories like that and put them in the Police Report."

The copy of the Broward County Police Report confirmed what the Broward County Sergeant and the Investigator of Internal affairs stated. **"There was no mention whatsoever of any jukeboxes being given by Robert to a Broward County family on the police report."** The Broward County Internal Affairs Investigator further reiterated, **"Officer xxxx did not say anything to the Lake County Detective about two jukeboxes being delivered to a family in Broward County by Robert O'Hare."**

Unfortunately, the conspiracy between the Lake County Prosecutor and the Lake County Detective xxxx of their bogus jukebox story worked, because the Judge xxxx, on March 20, 2017, denied reinstating my son's $25,000 bond, and wrote on his Order that Robert would be a danger to the Loch Leven community if released on Bond. The Judge further stated in his ruling; he used evidence submitted to him at the Bond Hearing, by the Lake County Detective XXXX.

Upon receiving the Judge's ruling, I made a formal complaint to the Lake County Internal Affairs against Detective xxxx for committing perjury and lying under oath about my son at the Bond Hearing. I submitted all the evidence from Broward County Internal Affairs Report, and included an article I found on the Detective's former arrest record for exposing his private parts in public. Upon reviewing my complaint, no charges were brought against Detective xxx by the Lake County Sheriff or the Lake County Internal Affairs.

Robert's defense team continued with their-preparation to fight the original charges stemming from the unlawful warrantless entry and illegal search of our home. They stated their case against the Deputies' criminal violations to Robert's 4th Amendment rights and Federal Statute 42 U.S.C. § 1983, was established by law. Therefore, according to Robert's 4th Amendment Rights, any evidence discovered during the Deputies' illegal search could not be used against Robert in a trial.

All that was needed was for the Judge to rule in favor of Robert's Motion to Suppress, which was based solely on the Deputies violation of Robert's 4th Amendment Rights to the U.S. Constitution. A Motion to Suppress is simply a formal request by a defendant that the judge excludes certain evidence from trial.

The Lake County Prosecutor knew, based on the evidence at hand, that the Motion to Suppress was likely to be granted. He knew that all evidence from the illegal search of our home could not be used and that he would have to dismiss the charges against Robert, and my son would be set free. This was when the Prosecutor began the highly unethical practice of postponing this inevitable Motion to Suppress Hearing from occurring. He was informed that Robert was terminal with stage four malignant colon cancer, that was advancing throughout his vital organs, the prosecutor purposefully stalled five Motions to Suppress Hearing dates for a period close to eight months: The original Hearing date was set on April 2017 then canceled and rescheduled for June 2017; then canceled and rescheduled for August 10, 2017; then canceled and rescheduled for September 5, 2017; then canceled and rescheduled for October 4, 2017; then canceled and rescheduled on November 8, 2017.

On November 8, 2017, the Hearing Date for the Motion to Suppress, the Prosecutor continued to exhibit egregious prosecutorial misconduct. The live video taken from my cell phone of the Deputies' violations was given to the Prosecutor to give to the Judge pre-hearing and for him to bring it to the Hearing. There was no logistical reason for this not happening because the Prosecutor's office was right next to the Judge's office in the same Court House Building.

However, upon reviewing the cell phone video, the Prosecutor knew this was damning evidence to his case. This video showed the deputies' unlawful entry, illegal search and seizure, and the aftermath of their severe beating to Robert. The Prosecutor intentionally showed up at the Motion to Suppress Hearing without the video. This video was Robert's most essential evidence to win his Motion to Suppress.

Fortunately, Robert's attorney suspected that the Prosecutor would not bring the video to the hearing as he promised. So, he brought to the Hearing an extra copy of the video file to present to the Judge. This left the Judge little or no chance to ignore the horrendous unlawful acts of the deputies.

We had to wait another month to receive the Judge's ruling on the Suppression Hearing. On December 4, 2017, the Judge wrote, "The court observes that no justification was offered as to why police did not seek a warrant prior to approaching the defendant's house for the knock and talk. Multiple search warrants had already been granted in the course of the investigation, nor does there appear to have been any particular time constraint. Had officers simply sought a warrant before entering the defendant's residence instead of afterward, they would have avoided an entirely unnecessary expenditure of both judicial and police resources. Separately from whether the tactics employed by police were legal, they were clearly unwise and unnecessary."

However, despite all this evidence, the Judge, in error, added to his Order, a Doctrine of Inevitable Discovery, which was not applicable to the Florida Supreme Court Case Law, Rodriguez vs. the State of Florida, which Robert's defense was based on. This Doctrine of Inevitable Discovery exonerated the deputies' warrantless search and unlawful seizure and caused Robert to lose his Motion to Suppress unjustly.

During the Proceedings, the Prosecutor lied to the Judge by misrepresenting the doctrine of Inevitable Discovery. This forced Robert's Trial Attorney to verbally chastise the Prosecutor in front of the Judge stating, "XXXX, if you lie one more time in Court, I will go after your Bar License." Robert's Attorney then presented the Judge with a copy of this case law, which clearly states in black and white that a Doctrine of Inevitable Discovery does not apply to the circumstances surrounding the Deputies warrantless search and seizure in our home. The Judge's bias against my son and for the Deputies caused him to ignore Supreme Court Case Law, and added this non-applicable Doctrine of Inevitable Discovery to his Final Order. Robert's defense team, knowing this could happen, had already prepared a Motion for Reconsideration to allow the Judge the opportunity to correct his error. Instead of correcting his error, the Judge denied the motion without adding any legal explanation.

Robert losing the Motion to Suppress meant that he would remain incarcerated without receiving any medical treatment for his malignant colon cancer. Ironically, it did give Robert the legal foothold to pursue an appeal and have the Judge's ruling reviewed by a higher court without the shadow of corruption that blanketed the Lake County Criminal Justice System.

This level of corruption caused me to sell our beautiful Mt. Dora, FL, home on November 16, 2017, and permanently move away from Lake County, back to our home in Fort Lauderdale, Fl.

ROBERT IS DIAGNOSED WITH TERMINAL STAGE 4 MALIGNANT COLON CANCER

Immediately following Robert's severe beating at the hands and feet of the Lake County Sheriff's Deputies on October 5, 2015, he suffered debilitating health issues which included: severe abdominal pain, blindness in his left eye, pain on the left side of his ribs, rectal bleeding, and difficulty eliminating bowel movements. These health issues were exacerbated after the Lake County Prosecutor filed 2nd Bogus charges against him, accusing Robert of delivering 2 Jukeboxes to a family in either 2011 or 2012 for the purpose of voyeurism. This false ridiculous charge was made up by the Prosecutor with absolutely no evidence whatsoever.

On August 17, 2016, when Robert and I left our Ft. Lauderdale residence, we were stopped by the U. S. Marshal who were executing the Lake County Prosecutor's warrant. They asked Robert to get out of the car and lie face down on the pavement. Then the officer abruptly pulled Robert's right arm up in the air, lifting him off the pavement bodily, then dropped him flat on his face on the concrete. From this brutal act, Robert landed on the hot pavement flat on his abdomen. Just then another officer laid bodily across Robert's left shoulder and said, "Put your hands behind your back." Robert put his right hand behind his back, but with the officer's full body weight laying on his left shoulder and his left arm underneath his chest, this was difficult to do. Despite the pain he forced his left arm from underneath his chest to put behind his back to comply with the officer's command. This caused his left arm and hands to be scratched and bloodied by the concrete.

This brutal abuse caused increased trauma to Robert's abdominal area. As the U.S. Marshals were putting Robert into their vehicle, he informed them that he was experiencing extreme abdominal pain. They took my son to the Emergency Room at the Broward Health Medical Center in Ft. Lauderdale, FL, for observation. The Broward Health's medical report, dated August 25, 2016, stated that my son had pre-cancerous bleeding polyps and should be seen by a Gastro-Intestinal (GI) Doctor within three days and must have a colonoscopy.

In addition to feeling nauseous and tired all the time, Robert lost a lot of weight in the Lake County Detention Center. For the first 2 1/2 months, he was incarcerated in a cell 24/7 and only allowed out of his cell for a total of 3 hours a week. Shortly thereafter, he weighed in at 145 pounds, down from his original weight of 190 pounds. While on lockdown, Robert drank unfiltered water from his cell that had a horrible taste and a foul odor. These conditions exacerbated his bowel and intestinal problems.

During his first thirteen months of incarceration, the Lake County Detention Center refused to give Robert any medical treatment from a GI doctor for his pre-cancerous bleeding polyps as prescribed by his medical report from the Broward Health Hospital. After making countless notifications to the Lake County Sheriff, the Lake County Warden, the Lake County State Attorney, and the Lake County Judge, they all ignored Robert's urgent need for medical treatment.

Robert's Lead Attorney visited him at the Lake County Detention Center and witnessed how ill he looked. Fearing for Robert's life, he made another Emergency Motion to the Lake County Judge for an outside medical furlough in September 2017. This time, the Judge allowed Robert one outside exam, with a Doctor in Leesburg, FL., for which I was asked to pay. Robert was accompanied to this medical appointment by two armed guards from the Lake County Detention Center, with chains around his waist and ankles. This was his first examination in the thirteen months since his incarceration on August 25, 2016.

This Doctor medically diagnosed Robert with colon cancer and inflammation of the pancreas and stated this condition was caused by an injury to his abdomen. This injury was caused by the Lake County Deputy, who repeatedly kicked Robert 10-12 times in his ribs and abdomen on October 5, 2015. The symptoms created from this beating were ongoing, which included blindness, pain, intestinal bleeding, nausea, weakness, and difficulties in moving his bowels.

Upon receiving the Doctor's medical report, the Lake County Detention Center called his Leesburg, FL office to terminate all medical care on Robert because they were going to have their own Doctor from the Detention Center treat him for his colon cancer. I was informed of this by the GI Doctor's Head Nurse.

Several days later, Robert was examined by the Detention Center's Oncologist, who gave Robert a colonoscopy. This test confirmed Robert has stage 4 malignant colon cancer with over a 70% blockage in his colon. The Detention Center failed to conduct any required tests, allowing Robert to suffer for the entire year. This was confirmed by the Doctor who stated to Robert and also put this in his Medical Report, "This cancer was present in your body for one year." He told Robert, the cancerous growth was so large in his colon he could not safely remove it without first using chemotherapy to shrink it, and said he needed an MRI to see the size of the cancer. The Detention Center said they would only allow him to have outside chemotherapy without hospitalization and wanted him to sign a waiver, freeing the Detention Center from any liability. Robert refused to sign their waiver.

On October 4th, 2017, our attorney made another Emergency Motion for a Medical Furlough to the Lake County Judge to get outside medical treatment. His ruling came immediately, "I deny your Motion. You can come back in another month to see if the Detention Center can supply your cancer treatments." The Judge made this ruling with full knowledge that the Detention Center had not given Robert any care or treatment for his cancer for over one year, and now wanted Robert to wait still another month with his current health crisis. His bias and unjust rulings were unconscionable.

After more than thirteen months of incarceration, the Lake County Judge had only allowed Robert a single outside visit to a GI doctor, and then only after he became critically ill. The only thing my son was receiving at the Lake County Detention Center up to that date was one iron pill per day for anemia due to his constant colon bleeding, and a stool softener so he could move his bowels, which often took up to 4 days. Robert told me he has to walk daily within the facility to be able to move his bowels as well as taking the stool softener.

The following day, October 5, 2017, the original, Leesburg, FL GI Doctor's surgical coordinator informed me of the following: "The doctor requested an MRI for Robert over one month ago, to see how large the cancerous growth was, so he could either operate or do chemotherapy. The MRI will show the size of the cancer to either surgically remove it or to immediately commence chemotherapy to reduce the size of the growth before surgery. If it's too large, the doctor can't operate unless the growth can be reduced in size." She added, "The Lake County Detention Center has dropped the ball."

She gave me the name of the Medical Treatment Coordinator for the Lake County Detention Center. She reiterated again, "Your son needs this taken care of immediately. Your son needs tests and an MRI to see the size of the cancer. This must be done immediately! No judge in the world will deny a person with your son's medical condition, a medical furlough."

Unfortunately, the Lake County Judge handling Robert's case was the one Judge in the world who did deny my son his Motion for a Medical Furlough for his urgently needed outside cancer treatment. He did this with the fully documented medical report as to the urgency for Robert to have immediate medical treatment.

During his continued incarceration at the Lake County Detention Center, Robert fell on his face repeatedly during his showers from being faint and weak due to anemia. On one occasion, a guard asked Robert as he exited the shower area if he had fallen again because his face was all red. Robert simply answered, "Yes."

Other inmates told Robert, "You look really bad, you look like you're dying. You have no color to your face; your skin is all gray." His attorney told him the same thing, "Robert, you look God awful." Fearing for Robert's life, the Attorney made multiple Emergency Motions to the Lake County Judge for Robert to receive urgently needed, outside medical treatment. The Lake County Judge denied all Motions for outside medical treatment.

The Lake County Detention Center did not give Robert any further tests or treatment for five months. It wasn't until January 28th, 2018, almost eighteen months after his incarceration date, that Robert was finally given five radiation treatments. The radiation treatments caused around the clock pain, suffering, and diarrhea. Robert couldn't hold his bowel movements and was confined 24/7 in a lock-down cell, and only allowed out three hours a week with no medical care or follow up treatment from a doctor. This maltreatment goes beyond being egregious against any human being, especially one who is critically ill and not being properly medically treated for stage 4 malignant colon cancer!

ROBERT'S QUEST FOR JUSTICE THROUGH A CORRUPT LAKE COUNTY JUDICIAL SYSTEM

On January 16, 2018, the Deputy who had repeatedly kicked Robert in the stomach 10-12 times on October 5, 2015, and lied under oath about him at his hearings, came to see him at the Lake County Detention Center. He told Robert he wanted to talk to him and ask some questions. He asked Robert, "Where are you going to live when you get out?" Robert refused to talk with him without his lawyers being present. This made the Deputy very angry. He ordered Robert into his cell, and he searched everything Robert had. He left with two bags of Robert's commissary food and one cookie. The guard on duty later came over to Robert and said, "I've been a guard here for 12 years, and I have never seen anything like this happen before to anyone. This Deputy was really pissed at you, Robert!"

Four days before the Deputy's visit to my son, he came to my home in Ft. Lauderdale, which is four hours from the Sheriff's office in Tavares, Fl. He banged on my front door for three hours and called me repeatedly on my cell phone from 3:45 pm to 6:45 pm until he finally left. Due to the fear of this Deputy banging on my door and repeatedly calling me, I phoned our Attorney, who looked up the number I gave him that was on my caller ID. He confirmed the number was registered to this Deputy. It was that same fear from the ongoing criminal and violent acts committed by the three Lake County Deputies, including their lying under oath at my son's hearings, that caused me to sell our home in Mt. Dora, FL, just months earlier.

Robert's lawyers counseled him not to go to trial with a biased judge, a corrupt prosecutor, and the lying deputies. They strongly recommended that he enter a plea of "No Contest" and Appeal the Judge's misinterpretation of the Supreme Court Case Law. By the Judge adding in a doctrine of Inevitable Discovery that shielded the Deputies violations. When his error was brought to his attention in a Motion for Reconsideration, the Judge refused to correct his error.

In pleading "No Contest," Robert would finally be free from the Lake County Judge's bias, dirty politics, unjust rulings, and the Prosecutor's collusion with the Deputies. Robert heeded the advice from his lawyers and took a plea because he had terminal malignant colon cancer and wanted to clear his name and win the appeal before anything happened to him. The Lawyers all agreed that the Appeal could get Robert the much-needed Justice he is legally entitled to as a US citizen.

Upon pleading "No Contest," the Lake County Judge immediately sentenced Robert to 20 years in a Florida State Correctional Facility. This sentence proved not only the Judge's bias but his unfair ruling against Robert's legal rights.

Expecting the Judge to deny their Motion for Reconsideration, Robert's lawyers had already prepared their Appeal Brief. Once Robert entered his "No Contest" plea, they were able to file for a supersedeas bond hearing. A supersedeas bond is a legal instrument that prevents a judgment from being executed while the defendant is appealing the decision.

On January 29, 2018, the eve of Robert's supersedeas bond hearing, the Lake County Prosecutor sank to a level of prosecutorial misconduct that I could never have imagined, even from someone with his past record! He filed another false charge against Robert of solicitation to kill the Lake County Judge! This new charge was based on an alleged conversation between Robert and me on a monitored jail call. This false and outlandish charge was made up, in my opinion, because the Prosecutor knew that the Appellate Court would reverse the Lake County Judge's Order to deny the Motion to Suppress, and he would have no choice but to dismiss all charges against Robert and set him free. **On February 1, 2019, an Appellate Court did reverse the Judge's order.**

The same Deputy who beat up my son and kicked him multiple times in the ribs and stomach on his forced entry into our home on October 5, 2015, was the one who was put in charge of the investigation. He publicly alleged to the news media the falsehood that Robert used a "secret code" to ask me to hire a long-time family friend to kill the Lake County Judge. This never happened!!!

This longtime family friend, a 76-year-old senior citizen, with a pacemaker, blind in one eye, cataracts in the other eye, was visited by this Detective at his home. He told the Deputy, "You are not going to do to my life what you did to Robert O'Hare. You Deputies have a very bad reputation in this community and are the ones that should be locked up, not the innocent people you go after." He also stated this to Robert's Lead Attorney and the news media. He said he told the Deputy, "I was never solicited to kill a judge. I have known Virginia and Robert for 35 years, and they wouldn't hurt anyone." He told me he wants to sue the Deputy and the Lake County Sheriff's office for smearing his name all over the news media with their bogus story.

These new false charges by the Sheriff's Office and the State Attorney's office were their final attempt to try to wash away their own criminal violations by putting their final nail in my son's coffin by falsely accusing Robert of such a charge on the eve of his supersedeas bond hearing. This new charge kept my son from being released on a new bond while keeping him incarcerated now for two years without any urgently needed medical treatment for his malignant colon cancer.

On January 11, 2018 this Deputy came to my home in Fort Lauderdale and banged on my door for 3 hours, then left because I refused to open my door to him. He also went to see Robert at the Lake County Detention Center on January 16, 2018. His first question to Robert was, "where are you going to live when you get out?" This showed his concern with Robert being set free. He monitored our jail calls and knew I was going to file a civil rights lawsuit against him. On September 2019 I did file a civil rights lawsuit against him and the entities involved in violating my son's civil and constitutional rights. This Federal civil rights lawsuit is scheduled for trial in early 2021.

Every American citizen has their Civil and Constitutional Rights from the moment we take our first breath when we come out of the birth canal until we take our last breath when our spirit returns to God who gave it. No American citizen, rich or poor, black or white, young or old, should ever settle for injustice, corruption, conspiracy, and bias from anyone employed by our Government that works in our Judicial System. Our constitutional rights are expressed in our Fifth Amendment guarantees that: "No person shall be deprived of life, liberty, or property, without due process of law." This applies to all states by the 14th Amendment.

Robert's lawyers had enough with dealing with the corruption, conspiracy, and bias from the Lake County Judicial System. One of Robert's Attorneys said, "I have never seen a case like this before in my entire career. With all this corruption, we will file a Motion to Recuse the entire Lake County Judicial System and defend these latest charges against Robert outside of the Lake County Judicial System."

In early February 2018, this motion was granted, and the Lake County State Attorney recused the Lake County Judge from my son's case.

Writing this book was gut-wrenching as I detailed all the corruption I witnessed in the Lake County Judicial System against my son. I only got through the heart-rendering details of the travesty of justice my son suffered through thus far, by being 100% inspired by God's Holy Spirit. I believe God is using my son's experience for me to write this book, "Virginia O'Hare Documents God's Laws vs. Man's Laws" to expose the corruption my son and I witnessed by Government Employees of the Lake County Florida Judicial System, and other entities involved in violating Robert's constitutional, civil and prisoner's rights.

Unfortunately, my beloved son, Robert Anthony, lost his battle for his life on July 27, 2020, at 8:40 PM from Stage 4 colon cancer while in our home under 24/7 Hospice care. Before his demise, the bogus charges against him, investigated by the Deputy who severely beat, kicked, and tore his shirt on that fateful day of October 5, 2015, were dropped by State Attorney Brad King on March 2, 2020. On January 23, 2020, A federal judge signed an order approving Robert's civil rights lawsuit going forward to trial on or about March 2021. He denied the Deputies Motion to Suppress, stating, "the individual claims asserted under section 1 and 2 are not dismissed." The Star Witness at trial for Robert Anthony will be his proud mother, Virginia O'Hare.

ROBERT ANTHONY O'HARE
1961 - 2020

Remembering Patty Lynne

Patty Lynne
Through the Years

1981 -
above - Anne Marie, Patty Lynne, and Virginia. A proud and beautiful mother with her two daughters.

left - Robert and Patty Lynne. Virginia's only son and youngest daughter.

1985 -
above and right - The entire family together celebrating Thanksgiving.

left - Viginia with her family at Christmas.

1987-
above - Virginia with Patty
Lynne *(l)* and Anne Marie *(r)*
at the Port of Ft. Lauderdale.

1989
left - Viginia and the girls at
home for Christmas.

1992-
above - Christmas with the family in our beautiful home in Ft. Lauderdale, Florida.

right - Viginia and Patty on Christmas night.

1997-
above - (l-r) Anne, Patty, Virginia, and Dan at a favorite restaurant.

2004
left - A beautiful mother and daughter moment for Virginia's birthday.

2008-
above - Virginia and her lovely daughter Patty Lynne.

2010
right - A very happy mother, Virginia, with her strong and beautiful daugher, Patty Lynne.

Israel & the Holy Land
1995

A beautiful family trip to Israel to experience the Holy Land.
(l-r) Anne Marie, Virginia, Dan, and Patty Lynne.

Baptism in the Jordan River

The entire family received baptism and rebirth in Jesus Christ in the Jordan River.

right - Patty receives prayer prior to baptism.

below - Patty rises from the waters of the Jordan River, Born Again and dedicated to Jesus Christ.

Church of the Nativity

above - Patty and Virginia lay hands on the very spot of our Lord and Savior, Jesus Christ's birth.

below - A very somber moment for Patty as she contemplates all of the Biblical sights and history of the Holy Land.

Ski Trip
Aspen, Colorado

right- Patty Lynne and longtime family friend, Al Bowman, prepare to hit the slopes in Aspen.

below - Patty bumps into Hollywood legend, Robert Wagner while relaxing in Aspen.